Understanding Dyscalculia and Numeracy Difficulties

of related interest

Practical Mathematics for Children with an Autism Spectrum Disorder and Other Developmental Delays
Jo Adkins and Sue Larkey
ISBN 978 1 84905 400 3
eISBN 978 0 85700 783 4

Can I tell you about Dyslexia?
A guide for friends, family and professionals
Alan M. Hultquist
ISBN 978 1 84905 952 7
eISBN 978 0 85700 810 7

How to Detect Developmental Delay and What to Do Next
Practical Interventions for Home and School
Mary Mountstephen
ISBN 978 1 84905 022 7
eISBN 978 0 85700 497 0

An Introduction to Dyslexia for Parents and Professionals
Alan M. Hultquist
JKP Essentials series
ISBN 978 1 84310 833 7
eISBN 978 1 84642 527 1

The Self-Help Guide for Teens with Dyslexia
Useful Stuff You May Not Learn at School
Alais Winton
ISBN 978 1 84905 649 6
eISBN 978 1 78450 144 0

Understanding
Dyscalculia
and
Numeracy Difficulties

A Guide for Parents, Teachers and Other Professionals

PATRICIA BABTIE AND JANE EMERSON

Jessica Kingsley *Publishers*
London and Philadelphia

First published in 2015
by Jessica Kingsley Publishers
73 Collier Street
London N1 9BE, UK
and
400 Market Street, Suite 400
Philadelphia, PA 19106, USA

www.jkp.com

Library of Congress Cataloging in Publication Data
A CIP catalog record for this book is available from the Library of Congress

British Library Cataloguing in Publication Data
A CIP catalogue record for this book is available from the British Library

ISBN 978 1 84905 390 7
eISBN 978 0 85700 754 4

Printed and bound in Great Britain

MIX
Paper from
responsible sources
FSC
www.fsc.org FSC® C013604

CONTENTS

PART 1

Overview of Numeracy Learning and Assessment

This book is about difficulties with numbers, which is not the same as a difficulty with mathematics. Numeracy is part of the branch of mathematics called arithmetic. While early numeracy problems may well put pupils off mathematics, it is important to be clear that number is only one aspect of mathematics. Mathematics is a vast subject that deals with pattern in its myriad forms.

Numeracy is an essential skill for life in the modern world. We are concerned with how to teach pupils who struggle to understand numbers, and too often give up. It may be obvious that a child has a problem because they cannot learn everyday sequences such as days of the week, or be able to count to 10, or they make errors in written calculations. (However, errors are an important part of learning, if pupils can work out *for themselves* what went wrong.) The problem may show up in written tests. The results of these assessments have three functions in schools: to show what a child knows, or does not know; to rank the children in terms of ability in the class; and to judge the child's performance against the curriculum requirements for that age.

Failure to achieve the appropriate level triggers alarm bells. What is the appropriate level for a particular child is a very tricky question because it involves judgements by adults about the child's ability and with expectations for learning based on that judgement. It is the belief of the authors of this book that all children in mainstream or community schools can learn basic numeracy and that it is essential to establish firm foundations in basic counting and calculation before moving on to larger numbers. This is not a view shared by all educationalists. However, it is an idea summed up in the US curriculum's Common Core Standards which are designed to address the problem of a curriculum that is 'a mile wide and an inch deep'. The difficulty arises when a child needs more time to assimilate ideas than the teaching pace allows; this is a difficult problem for classroom teachers and one where parents can help enormously.

The problem needs to be considered in the context of the education system. Children are taught in age cohorts. In the past children who failed to make sufficient progress were made to repeat the year. This had a negative impact on self-esteem which resulted in emotional and behavioural issues. Today pupils in many, but not all, countries move up each year to remain with their peers. However, being the same age does not mean that pupils will be at developmentally or cognitively similar levels. In a primary classroom children may well be functioning at completely different levels; in ordinary schools this may represent a gap of five years in attainment.

At this point it is worth considering some of the general underlying attitudes to maths, as these have a significant impact on expectations. Many pupils believe that they can't do maths because they are bad at maths. This attitude has prevailed in western countries for generations. Adults will readily admit: 'I can't do maths. I am not good at maths.' It would be unacceptable for adults in eastern countries to admit to this. The idea has grown up that some people are born with the ability to do maths and some are not. If this idea is logically extended it means that there is not much point in trying because 'I don't have the maths gene'. This is a pernicious idea and it is a fallacy. Developing number sense requires learning to look at the world and make sense of it. Becoming numerate is a complex process involving visual perceptual skills and language to develop numerical concepts. Learning about numbers is also intriguing, satisfying and exciting – even for those with difficulties, if they are allowed to develop their thinking and communication skills.

The first step is to identify where understanding has broken down. Next, plan a teaching programme which sets realistic goals to be achieved in a fixed time. Then use a multi-sensory approach to develop key number concepts such as counting, the principle of exchange and place value. Numeracy is a hierarchical subject in which one concept builds on another, so ensure that basic concepts are understood by moving at the pace of the child. Note that the goal is *understanding* rather than carrying out learned procedures. It is important that pupils are able to use standard methods; however, they also need to communicate their thinking using diagrams, charts, graphs and to explain it verbally. This can be difficult in a classroom situation, but failure to learn the basics leads on to persistent failure and a negative impact on adult life. Before looking at the details of how to teach so that children learn number sense, it is helpful to be clear about what is meant by numeracy, dyscalculia and specific learning difficulties (SpLD), and how children learn and remember before considering what can go wrong and make it difficult to learn.

Understanding Dyscalculia and Numeracy Difficulties consists of two parts:

Part 1: Overview of Numeracy Learning and Assessment

- overview of dyscalculia and numeracy learning difficulties

- background information about learning in general

- what is required to develop number sense and numeracy

- causes and indicators of numerical learning difficulties.

- the role of assessment in education

- identifying dyscalculia and numeracy difficulties.

Part 2: Teaching

- how to plan teaching starting by identifying where understanding has broken down

- overview of what to teach

- summary of how to teach using a multi-sensory approach

- how parents can help.

Quick facts about dyscalculia and numeracy difficulties

Dyscalculia is a specific learning difficulty which affects the most basic aspect of numeracy – learning to count. This in turn affects all numerical calculations.

Numeracy difficulties may be caused as a result of other specific learning difficulties. They may also occur for social, cultural and educational reasons.

Pupils can learn to become numerate if they are taught in a multi-sensory way and given time to think about what they see and describe it. Too often early numeracy is taught as an exercise in getting the correct answer as quickly as possible. Pupils do need to be able to calculate accurately; however, the modern world demands citizens who can do much more than be a human calculator; they need to be able to think and reason about numbers in order to use them to solve problems. They need to learn how to ask pertinent questions. Pupils need to be able to analyse information, to represent their thinking in diagrammatic ways as well as communicating their thinking succinctly using mathematical symbols.

1. What is dyscalculia?

    It is a condition that affects the ability to acquire arithmetical skills.

2. What are numeracy difficulties?

    Difficulties understanding the concept of number and the structure of the number system which leads to failure to acquire basic arithmetical skills at the age expected.

3. What are indicators of dyscalculia?

    A key indicator of dyscalculia is an inability to look at a small quantity of objects (less than 5) and say how many there are.[1]

---

[1] Use the word 'less', rather than 'fewer', in the early stages of teaching. Children often find the word 'fewer' difficult to understand. 'Less' means 'not as much'. It is used when referring to a total amount (the cardinal value). 'Fewer' means 'not as many'. It emphasizes the individual components of a number. The distinction need not be made until pupils can confidently use the terms 'more than' and 'less than'.

4. What are indicators of numeracy difficulties?

    Counting errors, difficulty learning key facts (bonds of numbers to 10) and lack of knowledge of place value.

5. What causes dyscalculia and numeracy difficulties?

    Dyscalculia is neurological in origin and is a deficit in the core capacity to process numbers. Numeracy difficulties may be caused by co-occurring specific learning difficulties. Difficulties may arise from developmental or visual perceptual factors which mean that the child is not ready to learn at the expected pace. They may also have social causes such as poverty and lack of life experience. Anxiety is a major cause of numeracy learning difficulties.

6. How common is dyscalculia?

    About 5 per cent of school-age children are estimated to have dyscalculia.

7. How common are numeracy difficulties?

    Severe numeracy difficulties affect about 25 per cent of the population in the UK.

8. Can dyscalculia be cured?

    Dyscalculia is not a disease, therefore it cannot be cured. Pupils with dyscalculia can learn to cope with numbers if they are taught appropriately. Dyscalculia affects the area of mathematics that deals with numbers (arithmetic). Pupils with dyscalculia can become competent in other areas of mathematics.

9. Can numeracy difficulties be cured?

    Pupils with numeracy difficulties can develop numeracy if they are allowed to proceed at the pace that is appropriate for them. They need to learn using multi-sensory methods and talk about what they are doing and thinking.

Dyscalculia, Numeracy Difficulties and Specific Learning Difficulties

Definitions

Learning difficulties are defined in terms of deficits or discrepancies as measured against specified criteria which might include standardized tests. So you need to establish what those 'correct' criteria are before you can consider what has gone wrong. There is also the question of the use of the words 'difficulty' and 'disability' which are used in different ways in different countries. The definitions of these terms have important implications for who provides remediation, including who pays for it.

Numeracy

Numeracy is an essential skill in the modern world. Numeracy is part of the branch of mathematics called arithmetic. Numerate people understand what numbers represent, how they are related to each other and how to use them to solve problems. The basis of numeracy is 'number sense', which is the ability to to understand and manipulate quantities.

> Numeracy is a life skill. Being numerate goes beyond simply 'doing sums'; it means having the confidence and competence to use numbers and think mathematically in everyday life... Being numerate is about appreciating number relationships and interpreting answers, and not just about doing calculations.
>
> (National Numeracy 2013)

Dyscalculia

Dyscalculia is a specific learning difficulty affecting number. It is neurological in origin and is a deficit in the core capacity to process numbers. This manifests itself as an inability to compare and enumerate small quantities, which leads to difficulty acquiring basic numeracy (Butterworth 1999; Dehaene 1997; Simmons 2008). People with dyscalculia have intelligence at least within the average: the difficulty specifically affects their ability to understand numbers.

A distinction is made between developmental dyscalculia, which is present at birth, and acquired dyscalculia, which is caused by brain injury. 'Developmental dyscalculia is usually and rather broadly defined as a low mathematical achievement in the presence of otherwise normal intelligence and access to educational resources' (Mareschal, Butterworth and Tolmie 2013, p.215).

The UK Department for Education and Skills (DfES) clearly outlined the difficulties in the definition in the National Numeracy Strategy in 2001.

> Developmental dyscalculia is a condition that affects the ability to acquire arithmetical skills. Dyscalculic learners may have difficulty understanding simple number concepts, lack an intuitive grasp of numbers, and have problems learning number facts and procedures. Even if they produce a correct answer or use a correct method, they may do so mechanically and without confidence.

> (Department for Education and Skills 2001)

Cognitive neuroscientists define dyscalculia as a difficulty with number which has a specific neurological cause. It is important to be clear that dyscalculia is a difficulty that affects numeracy; it is not a difficulty with mathematics except for the areas of mathematics that deal with number. Of course many of the reasoning skills that are developed through learning arithmetic are transferable to other areas of mathematics. For example, it is not possible to enumerate the number of sides of a polygon if you cannot count accurately.

Dyscalculia and numeracy difficulties

Understanding what different people mean by the term dyscalculia turns out to be much more difficult than simply saying that it is a difficulty affecting number sense. The word dyscalculia is often used as an umbrella term to describe a wide range of difficulties with mathematics.

There are many factors, other than dyscalculia, that cause difficulty acquiring numeracy. These include conditions such as dyslexia, dyspraxia, attention deficit disorder (ADD) and attention deficit hyperactivity disorder (ADHD). Each of these can cause numeracy difficulties, or they may co-occur with dyscalculia. More general cognitive difficulties such as visual-spatial processing and language processing contribute to numeracy difficulties. Social and economic factors play a significant role. Emotional factors also affect progress: pupils who enjoy the subject and believe they can do it are likely to persevere with challenges and hence improve their knowledge. Those who do not are more likely to fail as a result of giving up trying and may develop maths anxiety which can prevent any learning taking place. This is discussed in more detail in Chapter 2.

Other terms may be used instead of dyscalculia, such as mathematics learning disability, or specific arithmetical learning difficulty. Underlying all the definitions is the notion of a failure to acquire particular academic skills related to numeracy at the expected age. Children are deemed to have a specific learning difficulty if their intelligence is at least in the average range but their performance is well below that expected for their age and ability.

The definitions provided in the *International Classification of Diseases-10* (Diagnosis Code F81.2) (World Health Organization 2010) known as the ICD-10, and in *The Diagnostic and Statistical Manual of Mental Disorders* (DSM-5 Diagnostic Code 315.1) (American Psychiatric Association 2013) are particularly important as these manuals are used throughout the world as the standards on which diagnostic decisions are made. The ICD-10 is produced by the World Health Organization and the DSM-5 is compiled by the

American Psychiatric Association. DSM-5 is the latest edition of the manual and was released in 2013. It is worth noting that there has been considerable criticism of the new definitions affecting learning difficulties in DSM-5 (Colker *et al.* 2012).

Do the differences in definitions matter? The purpose of a diagnosis is to establish what is wrong in order to be able to remediate the problem. The fact that diagnosis of specific learning difficulties falls under the psychiatric branch of medicine may surprise, even alarm, some parents. It is interesting that the criteria for diagnosis depends on failure to perform on a particular kind of academic test usually requiring recall of information at speed and communication in written form. As researchers at Yale University point out: 'To relegate the diagnosis of dyslexia or related learning disorders to only those who have failed, shows a serious lack of understanding of both the scientific and clinical aspects of learning disorders' (Colker *et al.* 2012, p.10).

Special educational needs and disabilities (SEND)

Dyscalculia falls into the category of special educational needs (SEN) (cognition and learning) for education purposes. Pupils with SEN are entitled, by law, to have appropriate teaching to help them to learn. Major changes to SEN provision in the UK were introduced in 2014 by aligning education, health and welfare needs. The changes are intended to simplify the process and parents are expected to take a more active role in their child's education and well-being. Class teaching is expected to be more inclusive and meet the needs of all the children in the class. The aim is to reduce the need for SEN interventions outside the classroom. The Dyslexia-SpLD Trust provides comprehensive guidance about he educational changes at www.thedyslexia-spldtrust.org.uk.

The *Special Educational Needs and Disability Code of Practice: 0 to 25 years* (Department for Education and Department of Health 2015) gives the following guidance:

Special educational needs (SEN)

xiii. A child or young person has SEN if they have a learning difficulty or disability which calls for special educational provision to be made for him or her.

xiv. A child of compulsory school age or a young person has a learning difficulty or disability if he or she:

- **has a significantly greater difficulty in learning than the majority of others of the same age,** or

- has a disability which prevents or hinders him or her from making use of facilities of a kind generally provided for others of the same age in mainstream schools or mainstream post-16 institutions

xv. For children aged two or more, special educational provision is educational or training provision that is **additional to or different from that made generally for other children or young people of the same age by mainstream schools**, maintained nursery schools, mainstream post-16 institutions or by relevant early years providers. For a child under two years of age, special educational provision means educational provision of any kind.

xvi. A child under compulsory school age has special educational needs if he or she is likely to fall within the definition in paragraph xiv. above when they reach compulsory school age or would do so if special educational provision was not made for them (Section 20 Children and Families Act 2014).

xvii. Post-16 institutions often use the term learning difficulties and disabilities (LDD). The term SEN is used in this Code across the 0–25 age range but includes LDD.

(Department for Education and Department of Health 2015, pp.15–16)

This is a very broad definition and gets around the problem of whether there is a difference between a difficulty and a disability by using both terms. However, there is considerable disagreement about how the words are used in clinical practice and they are used in different ways in different countries.

In the UK the term 'specific learning difficulties' (SpLD) is used to cover those difficulties and disabilities that affect the way information is learned and processed. In the US the term 'learning disability' may be used instead of SpLD. Specific learning difficulties exist on a continuum from mild to moderate through to severe. SLDs have a neurological (not a psychological) origin and occur in people with average or above average intelligence.

Intelligence is measured using standardized tests to obtain an intelligence quotient (IQ) score where the average range is usually a score of between 90 and 110 points. There is a grey area between 70 and 90 points as the scores can be skewed by individual test items. People with an IQ score of about 50 or below are deemed to have an intellectual difficulty meaning that there are global difficulties rather than specific difficulties. The term 'mental retardation' has been replaced by the term 'intellectual disability (intellectual developmental disorder)' in DSM-5 (diagnostic code 319). The new guidelines make it clear that IQ score is only one factor to consider when making a diagnosis; it needs to be considered within the whole context of the person's life.

Terminology matters because it affects the way that help is provided and paid for. In the UK schools are responsible for identifying pupils with potential special educational needs and have to provide appropriate educational support funded from the school's budget. If the pupil does not make progress and additional help is required, the education authority may pay top-up funding. Where there are complex needs, a pupil will need to be formally assessed to find out if they qualify for an Education, Health and Care Plan (EHCP). The EHCP is a document that sets out the pupil's special educational needs and the help that is required to meet those needs. In September 2014 the EHCP replaced the Statement of Special Educational Needs. This will be discussed in more detail in Chapter 5.

CHAPTER 2

How Pupils Learn

It is helpful to consider how children learn before discussing the problems that occur when they have difficulty learning. There has been much debate over the years about different theories of learning and no doubt it will continue as new research tools are developed. In the past researchers' primary method of investigating how people learnt was by observation and asking them what they were thinking. Now cognitive neuroscientists can 'watch' brain activity as it takes place by using powerful neuro-imaging tools. They have identified neural networks that clearly link visual recognition with speech and with word meanings that enable people to read. They have identified specific areas in the brain, and the networks between them, that are involved with understanding numbers. Cognitive neuroscientists are also able to consider more general aspects of cognitive processes such as memory, visual perception and visuo-spatial skills as well as other important factors including attention, motivation, social and emotional development (Mareschal *et al.* 2013).

It is obvious that people have different intellectual abilities. What causes intellectual differences? The answer to that question involves an ongoing debate as to whether intelligence is a genetic trait that you are born with, or a capacity, influenced by your environment, that can be developed. The debate is sometimes referred to as nature versus nurture. Today there is general (but not total) agreement that both genes and the environment influence intellectual development.

What does cause intellectual differences? This sounds an innocuous question; it is not. Governments base social and educational policies on the answer. In the past, the answer to the question 'What causes intellectual differences?' led to some appalling injustices to individuals and whole groups of people.

The belief that intellectual differences are caused by gender led to women being denied higher education and the right to vote; they were deemed intellectually inferior to men. In the 1800s the medical profession in Britain and America strongly advised against higher education for women because of the detrimental effect on their health. In England, one of the most influential psychiatrists of the time was Henry Maudsley. Writing in 1874 he said that girls who were subjected to the same education as boys were in danger of being 'seriously deranged'. He quoted research by the Boston physician Dr Edward Clarke that found that 'an excessive educational strain' had led to a 'number of female graduates of schools and colleges who have been permanently disabled to a greater or less degree by improper methods of study' (Maudsley 1874, p.206).

The belief that intellectual differences are caused by race led to educational discrimination. Genetic explanations of racial differences in educational achievement were widespread in many parts of the world well into the 20th century. The racist view that blacks are inherently inferior to whites led to separate education for African Americans. The law only started to change with the landmark legal case Brown vs Board of Education in 1954.

In South Africa the belief in the inherent inferiority of people with black skins caused even worse injustices. A pillar of the apartheid system which denied human rights to black South Africans was the Black Education Act 1953. The apartheid system was based on the idea that black people were 'naturally' inferior to white people. It explicitly denied a mathematical education to black children to ensure that they remained economically disadvantaged. Speaking in Parliament in 1953, Dr Verwoerd, prime minister of South Africa, said: 'What is the use of teaching the (black) child mathematics when it cannot use it in practice? What is the use of subjecting a (black) child to a curriculum which, in the first instance, is traditionally European?' (Suzman 1993).

Examples of education denied on spurious lines of inherited traits have occurred in many countries throughout history and still blight children's life chances. The recent award of the Nobel Prize to Malala Yousafzai highlighted the fact that girls may still be denied education on gender lines.

The brain: neurons, currents, electricity and myelination

Many different areas of the brain are involved as the person explores the world using their senses of touch, sight, hearing, smell and taste. Thinking takes place as new information is integrated with knowledge that is already stored in memory. Visual perception and language play a central role in the process.

Each human brain has billions of neurons which are connected into neural pathways. Neurons communicate with one another at the synapses where there is a minute gap. It is here that a chemical change occurs which causes an electrical current to travel along the neurons.

As the current passes along a neuron, a substance called myelin forms a sheath around the part of the neuron called the axon. The myelin sheath is essential for learning. Each time the electrical current passes along the neural pathway, the myelin gets thicker and this helps speed up the signals. The stronger the connections, and the more areas of the brain are connected, the more enduring and useful the memory is. This is why multi-sensory learning is so important – it involves movement, visuo-spatial and auditory brain circuits and helps to build meaningful concepts.

There are many factors involved in brain and cognitive development, including genetics, nutrition, life experiences, physical activity, to name a few. There has long been a debate, often described as nature versus nurture, about the extent to which genes or environment affect learning. In fact they have a very complex interrelationship. It is more helpful to consider environmental factors. A healthy diet is helpful for brain development; whereas malnutrition leads to delays in motor and cognitive development. Positive life experiences in a nurturing environment promote brain development, whereas chronic stress in young children is associated with reduced brain size and can lead to lifelong difficulties.

Meaning and memory

Meaning plays an important part in memory. It is very difficult to remember something if it has no meaning *for you*. This is an important point in teaching. As adults we often assume that things we consider simple, such as learning the counting sequence, will be easy for children if they have enough repetition. Rote learning involves regular repetition of information, often in a rhythmic way, until it is remembered and can be quickly retrieved from memory. However, it is only useful if it can be applied.

Learning involves processing information that is taken in through the senses and stored in the brain in order to be used later. The information must be meaningful to you in order to remember it. The meaning may be wrong in terms of the general understanding, which is why it is so important that children construct meaning and concepts in mathematics from physical objects. Rote learning may result in erroneous information being stored. Memories that are securely lodged in the brain are difficult to dislodge. This is excellent if the meaning is correct; destructive if the meaning is wrong.

According to the psychologist Reuven Feverstein, the process of constructing a new memory, whether a concept, or formulating an idea, requires reflective thinking which involves three basic elements (Sharron and Coulter 1987):

- **perception** – something to think about

- **language** – it needs to be precise to be useful

- **time** – to develop, to think.

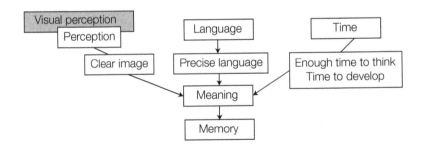

Perception

Our senses perceive stimuli using the five senses: sight, hearing, smell, taste and touch. The more of these senses that are involved in constructing an idea, the more neural pathways are activated and the more enduring the memory – provided that the information is processed efficiently and not merely activity for the sake of it.

Visual perception is particularly important for success in school. It is also essential for learning mathematics. Visual perception is how the brain deals with what it sees. A fairly sophisticated level of visual perception is assumed in the classroom. An immaturity in any of the visual perceptual components leads inevitably to difficulty laying down visual images and difficulty with many aspects of education (Portwood 2000).

Language

Language needs to be precise to be useful. A profuse stream of words may blind you to the fact that someone does not have command of language. Most of us use associative language: we describe objects, or explain ideas, by giving examples rather than being clear about the properties that define them. Mathematics requires precision in both thinking about and communicating ideas, an ability that develops gradually as pupils work with and discuss objects and ideas. It is important to realize that naming, or labelling, an object or an idea is the first stage in creating a visual image in the brain, one that will enable the child to think about it.

Spoken or written language is not the only way to communicate thought, especially in mathematics which uses pictures, diagrams, charts, graphs and numbers. However, you do need a verbal language to think logically, even if the conversation is a silent one with yourself. This is why it is important to use a multi-sensory approach to teach numeracy so that children learn to use language to interpret what they see. This process is sometimes referred to as visualization and verbalization and lies at the heart of teaching numeracy.

Time

Learning takes time. As discussed above, physical changes take place in the brain as you think. Thinking becomes more efficient as neural pathways are reinforced, but it does require time for this to happen. There are two aspects to this:

- time to think

- developmental maturation rate.

Thinking takes time. It involves being observant and focusing on information, analysing it and deciding what is relevant before comparing it with what is already known. Attempts to hurry the process increase stress, which may make it more difficult to think, or in extreme cases provoke such anxiety that the child stops thinking altogether.

Children's brains mature at different rates. It is very important in learning numeracy that children work at the level they are cognitively able to. Unfortunately, in schools children are sometimes expected to learn information that they are cognitively not ready to cope with. Children whose motor skills and visual perceptual skills are behind those expected in the classroom may become anxious, with resultant behavioural and emotional problems. This is likely to affect their ability to learn.

Adults should remember that it takes time to process auditory information. Instructions given too quickly may confound children on several fronts. They may not hear the words because they cannot distinguish the speech sounds. If they cannot process the information, they cannot remember the instruction. They may not have time to carry out the instruction before the next instruction is given.

It is important to take the time to speak clearly, and very important to take the time to listen to what the child has to say.

Memory

The memory process can be summarized as:

- take information into the brain

- keep it there

- get it out when required.

An enduring memory occurs when there is a clear mental image, labelled in such a way that it can be linked to other information in the brain and quickly recalled when required. This is particularly important in numeracy where existing knowledge is constantly required for work on new information.

Numeracy requires efficient memory. Memory requires linking to something you already know. In numeracy, new concepts are built on previous knowledge. Information needs to be taken in efficiently and stored in a systematic way so that it can be retrieved easily to apply to new tasks. It is important to revise information regularly to ensure it remains in long-term memory. The memory process is complex. Changes occur in the actual structure of the brain as new information is taken in and compared with what is already in memory.

It can be helpful to compare memory to a filing system: information is taken in, put in the correct place, then taken out when it is needed. A good filing system has clear categories which can be quickly accessed. It also means that the information going into it must be clear so it is easy to put it in the correct category, which requires working on the information.

Memory works in the same way: information is taken in through the senses, worked on, then stored in long-term memory. The difference between the brain and the filing system is that the existing memory is involved in working on the new information. There are three different kinds of memory: long-term, short-term and working memory.

Long-term memory

Information is stored in long-term memory so that it can be recalled and retrieved in the future. In numeracy this would include knowledge of essential facts, the structure of the number system, processes and procedures. The more that memory is reinforced, the longer it will endure.

Short-term memory

Information required for immediate use is held temporarily in short-term memory so that it is available to the working memory. An example that is often given is remembering a new telephone number; once it has been dialled, the number is forgotten as it does not need to be stored in long-term memory. Short-term memory is also involved in the reasoning process. It makes knowledge retrieved from the long-term memory available to the working memory.

Working memory

Working memory is the system which enables a person 'to hold in mind and mentally manipulate information over short periods of time' (Gathercole and Alloway 2007).

There are two aspects to working memory: auditory working memory and visual working memory. Auditory working memory is essential for understanding oral instructions and questions. The ears pick up spoken information which is either stored in short-term memory for immediate use, or stored in long-term memory.

Visual working memory is crucial for numeracy. It is involved with the interpretation, retention and manipulation of patterns, shapes and sequences (Alloway and Alloway 2010). Visual working memory enables people to think about non-verbal information, such as objects or pictures, and develop mental images which are then used to derive new ideas. Constructing visual images by working with concrete objects, talking about them and drawing diagrams of them, is an essential, but often neglected, part of learning numeracy.

Factors that affect learning
The basics

Sometimes educators overlook the most basic factors that affect learning – water, food, exercise and sleep. The brain requires enough water to function effectively. If a child is dehydrated their attention and memory will be affected. Brains also require adequate nutrients from a balanced diet. Exercise is important both for physical health and for cognitive development. It is through movement that motor skills, directional and visuo-spatial abilities are developed and these are prerequisites for learning to become literate and numerate. Another benefit of exercise is emotional well-being, as it reduces stress, something which is becoming an increasing problem for children in the modern world. The brain requires sufficient rest in order to function effectively.

Language

Numeracy has a language of its own, that is unique to learning about numbers, how they relate to each other and which basic operations are applied in the early stages of building foundation skills. It is essential to teach the language of maths right from the outset so that pupils understand what is being studied and can also express themselves accurately using numerical terms.

Many young learners find learning the second decade numbers (11 to 20) very difficult as the basic numbers roots change: *three* changes to *thir*teen, *five* to *fif*teen and twenty is often confused with twelve.

Pupils with weak memories for acquiring new vocabulary struggle to remember that 'add', 'plus', as well as 'and', all relate to combining quantities together. Similarly, 'take away', 'minus' and 'subtract' can be confusing at first, with finding the difference between numbers adding to possible confusions. The vocabulary relating to multiplication and division can be similarly confusing, with the word 'times' being very poorly understood in the early stages. Many pupils with poor numeracy are fearful of division as a topic and will benefit from using more transparent language at first involving groups of items forming equal-sized sets when discussing division in the early stages.

It is important that the correct terms are taught right from the beginning so that pupils not only understand them but are able to use them accurately and with confidence. Word problems can be introduced orally from the start so that if pupils have weak literacy skills they are not held back with their maths vocabulary development. As their understanding of numbers grows they can be encouraged to regularly explain their thinking and show working that they can explain to others.

Attitudes and emotions

The attitude that a child has to learning has a significant effect on their progress. Children with a positive attitude are likely to do better. If they enjoy what they are doing, they do more of it so that they become more proficient. This sets up a virtuous cycle of learning. Because they do better they are encouraged to do more, and so they improve. There is some evidence that the feeling of happiness or pleasure results in better learning. The opposite is also true: a child who has a negative attitude to learning is likely to give up easily and avoid the task. This results in failure to learn, leading to increased reluctance to try and therefore less progress. Again this sets up a spiral of despair generating increasingly negative emotions such as unhappiness, stress and anxiety. Fear disrupts brain activity and may make it impossible to learn. It is really bad for children to fear maths, so it is very important to help them develop a positive attitude through patient teaching at an appropriate level.

Motivation

Helping children to become motivated is one of the main challenges facing all educators.

Motivation is the drive that causes us to act. It is a key ingredient in learning. Motivation may be defined as the process that initiates, guides and maintains goal-oriented behaviours. A person may be motivated by external factors such as rewards, prizes or praise from another person. This is known as extrinsic motivation. In contrast, internal motivation causes a person to do a task or behave in a particular way because it is personally rewarding to them. This is called intrinsic motivation. The pleasure of finding things out is an important motivator in learning mathematics.

Mindset

A person's mindset is their 'attitude or disposition that predetermines (their) responses to and interpretations of situations' (American

Heritage Dictionary 2011).[1] In groundbreaking research, Carol Dweck, a psychologist at Stanford University, coined the terms 'fixed mindset' and 'growth mindset' to describe the ways in which people approached tasks. Those with the 'fixed mindset' believe that intellectual capacity is something you are born with; those with the 'growth mindset' believe that you can improve your performance or skills by hard work. These differing views have profound effects on pupils' performance in some surprising ways.

Dweck found that there is 'no relation between students' abilities or intelligence and the development of mastery-oriented qualities' (Hopkins 2004). She also found that there is 'no relation between a history of success and seeking or coping with challenges… The ability to face challenges is not about your actual skills; it's about the mind-set you bring to a challenge.'

What Dweck did find was that students with a fixed mindset who are deemed 'smart' or 'clever' fare particularly badly when faced by difficult challenges; they are afraid of failing. In contrast, those with a 'growth mindset' who focus on learning rather than being concerned with proving how 'smart' they are, find difficult tasks interesting and believe that they can solve them if they persevere. When they experience a setback, they focus on effort and strategies instead of worrying that they are incompetent (Dweck 2006).

These findings have important implications for education. As Dweck said:

> Teaching students to value hard work, learning, and challenges; teaching them how to cope with disappointing performance by planning for new strategies and more effort; and providing them with the study skills that will put them more in charge of their own learning. In this way, educators can be highly demanding of students but not run the risk that large numbers of students will be labelled as failures.

> (Hopkins 2004)

---

1   Copyright © 2011 by Houghton Mifflin Harcourt Publishing Company. Adapted and reproduced by permission from The American Heritage Dictionary of the English Language, Fifth Edition.

Attention and focus

Successful learning requires attention and focus. The brain can only deal effectively with one thing at a time. Overstimulation can make it difficult, if not impossible, for a child to focus on a task. It is worth remembering this when children are in busy classrooms where they may be distracted by other children talking and colourful displays.

Executive function

Executive function is the term used to describe the mental abilities that we use to manage and regulate all our behaviour. It 'helps connect past experience with present action'. Executive function is essential for 'planning, organizing, strategizing, paying attention to and remembering details, and managing time and space' (Morin 2014).

Children develop executive function from their interaction with nurturing adults and a supportive environment. Three types of interrelated brain functions underpin the development of executive function and the associated self-regulation skills: working memory, mental flexibility and self-control.

- **Working memory** governs our ability to retain and manipulate distinct pieces of information over short periods of time.

- **Mental flexibility** helps us to sustain or shift attention in response to different demands or to apply different rules in different settings.

- **Self-control** enables us to set priorities and resist impulsive actions or responses.

(Center on the Developing Child 2004)

Learning styles

It has long been known that people learn in different ways. Over 2500 years ago Confucius wrote:

I hear and I forget.

I see and I remember.

I do and I understand.

The idea that people have different learning styles, and the implications of this for teaching, has generated a great deal of research, debate and controversy. Entering that debate is outside the scope of this book. There is controversy about the use of the term 'styles' to summarize the way that people learn. For the sake of simplicity, the term 'learning style' is taken to mean the preferred way of processing information about the world.

For hundreds of years academic success has been associated with the written word, or symbol, probably because the assessment of achievement is usually print based. This approach emphasizes a verbal way of thinking and learning. Now the world is changing and much complex information will be increasingly handled visually rather than verbally (West 2009). So much data is amassed daily on so many different topics that it is simply not possible to present and interpret it in traditional written and numerical ways. Graphs and computer graphics convey ideas more quickly and more meaningfully than pages of print. Dealing with these new ways of communication requires the visuo-spatial skills.

Some children learn in a different way – visually, kinaesthetically or practically. It is not simply a matter of seeing, touching and doing. 'It involves using your whole being, engaging all your senses to feel or imagine what is happening. Visual, aural and kinaesthetic learning are all intertwined; together they can lay down a memory – of movement, feeling, sight and sound – that will be recalled as a total experience, not just as a recited chant' (Clausen-May 2003, p.3).

The importance of visual and kinaesthetic learning in maths was recognized and systematized in the 1920s and 1930s by Dienes and Cuisenaire, and popularized by Gattegno in the 1950s. They developed systems of cuboids so that the physical objects represented the relative size of different quantities. These are used to demonstrate number concepts and relationships. However, this method of teaching fell out of favour in the latter part of the 20th century. It has recently been revived, notably in the Singapore maths curriculum which uses a bar method using similar principles to those described by Cuisenaire and Gattegno.

These principles may be summarised as concrete-pictorial-abstract. The pupil models the question, represents the information pictorially which may be a diagram or a graph, and then writes it using mathematical symbols.

The use of manipulatives was advocated in *Mathematics Count* (also known as the Cockcroft Report) which was an investigation into the teaching of mathematics in schools in the UK published in 1982. 'Throughout our report we have stressed the importance of practical experience at all stages of the mathematics course. **In order to provide such experience the necessary equipment must be available.** Much of what is required is neither elaborate nor expensive but it needs to be available in sufficient quantity and to be readily accessible.' (Cockcroft 1982 p.184 (point 608); emphasis in original) The report goes on to say that '**Practical equipment of similar kinds** [to that used in primary school] **should also be available in secondary schools**.'

Multiple intelligences

The theory of multiple intelligences was developed by Howard Gardner and published in the 1980s. It is based on the belief that there is not one single kind of intelligence that can be measured by standardized test. Instead Gardner proposed that there are eight distinct areas of intelligence including mathematical, visual and verbal. Strength (or weakness) in one intelligence does not predict strength (or weakness) in any other intelligences. Over time people came to conflate the idea of multiple intelligences with learning styles. Gardner strongly refutes this idea (Strauss 2013).

Mathematical thinking styles or personalities

The way that people see the world affects the way that they process and analyse information. Some people begin with the details and piece them together to make up the whole. Others start from the other direction. They see the 'big picture' and find the patterns contained within it. This is a simple way of describing different thinking styles that are often called mathematical personalities. These personalities exist on a continuum, with most people falling somewhere between the two extremes.

Various terms are used to describe the personalities. Terms for those who focus on the details are quantitative, analytic or linear thinkers; those who start with the 'big picture' may be called qualitative, visual or holistic thinkers. More memorable are the labels: inchworm and grasshopper (Chinn and Ashcroft 1993). The thinking styles need not be exclusive; good mathematicians are able both to analyse the detail and see the whole.

The characteristics of these personalities can be summarized as follows:

Quantitative, analytic, linear	Qualitative, visual, holistic
Sequential, procedural	Sees patterns and relationships
Deductive	Inductive
Prefers linguistic and numerical information rather than diagrams	Uses diagrammatic representations
Prescriptive in nature, classifies, categorizes	Forms parallel and subsidiary problems to see relationships

CHAPTER 3

What Is Numeracy?

Numeracy refers to the ability to make sense of numbers and to use them effectively in real-life situations. The basis of numeracy is number sense: understanding what numbers represent and how they can be used to solve problems.

> The key components of number sense…include an awareness of numbers and their uses in the world around us, a good sense of place value concepts, approximation, estimation, and magnitude, the concept of numeration, and an understanding of comparisons and the equivalence of different representations and forms of numbers.

> (New Jersey Mathematics Coalition 1996, p.176)

Number sense develops as children interact with the world and start making sense of it by exploring and chatting about what they see and do. The concept of number that gradually emerges involves recognizing the patterns and relationships between numbers, and the ability to use that understanding to derive new concepts and use the information to solve problems.

The cornerstone of number sense is the ability to subitize. This is an innate cognitive ability which enables a person to rapidly compare the size of two randomly scattered groups of objects (up to 4 or 5 objects). It is fundamental to learning to count. Once a person has learned to count, they can also instantly say how many are in the set *without counting*. This is different to estimation, which is the skill, developed with practice, to say *roughly* how many items there are in a group of more than 5 items *without counting*. (The lack of the ability to subitize is a key indicator of dyscalculia. Faced with 3 objects, the person with dyscalculia would have to count them, and even then would not be sure of the accuracy of the count.)

The researchers Back, Sayers and Andrews (2014) have suggested that there are two aspects to number sense: foundational number sense and applied number sense.

> Foundational number sense (FNS) concerns the number-related understandings children develop during the early years of formal instruction... Applied number sense, draws on [FNS] and concerns the number-related understanding necessary for people to be mathematically competent and functionally effective in society. (p.1835)

They researched definitions of number sense in research literature in different cultures and identified seven common elements:

1. an awareness of the relationship between number and quantity

2. an understanding of number symbols, vocabulary and meaning

3. the ability to engage in systematic counting, including notions of cardinality and ordinality

4. an awareness of magnitude, and comparisons between different magnitudes

5. an understanding of different representations of number

6. competence with simple mathematical operations

7. an awareness of number patterns including recognizing missing numbers.

This list is useful for teaching purposes because it reminds teachers of the importance of the foundations of number sense, which need to be constantly reinforced to develop conceptual understanding rather than merely teaching processes and procedures in isolation.

Basic numeracy skills

Basic numerical thinking requires the following knowledge and skills:

- **counting** accurately and flexibly

- understanding **number relationships**

- understanding **place value**

- **calculation** – problem solving that involves processing numbers or quantities to derive new information

- knowing **key facts** – bonds of numbers to 10, multiplication by 10

- the **generalizing from known facts** to derive new facts

- understanding the difference between the **counting numbers** and the **measuring numbers**

- **numerical thinking** – reason logically to analyse numerical information in order to solve problems and communicate ideas in a variety of ways including diagrammatic, graphical and symbolic

Counting

Our understanding of a number is closely aligned to counting. The foundation of numeracy is the ability to count accurately and fluently with understanding. Counting is the action of finding the number of objects in a set (cardinal value). Counting also identifies the position in a sequence (ordinal aspect).

THE PRINCIPLES OF COUNTING

Gelman and Gallistel (1978) listed five principles of counting:

1. The one-one principle, also known as one-to-one correspondence.
    One number name (or 'tag') is assigned to each item counted.

2. The stable-order principle.
    The count words (one, two, three...) have to be used in a particular order to form the counting sequence.

3. The cardinal principle.
    The number assigned to the final object in the count represents the total quantity of objects in the set. This is also called the numerosity of the set.

4. The abstraction principle.
    Any collection of objects can be counted whether they are physically present or imaginary.

5. The order-irrelevance principle.
    The order in which the objects are counted does not matter, as long as every item is counted only once.

Number relationships

Relationships exist between numbers and within numbers. Exploring the similarities and differences between numbers leads to seeing the connections between them, and uncovers the patterns within numbers. These relationships include comparison, part–whole relationships, base-10 relationships and the relationships between the numerical operations. Pupils who fail to see the internal structures within numbers conceive of numbers as 'clumps' of ones, which leads to failure to learn to calculate. Working with concrete materials helps pupils visualize the relationships and develop a conceptual understanding.

COMPARISON

This is the ability to compare quantities in terms of size, meaning the number in the collection. Understanding comparison is important for developing effective calculation strategies and for representing numbers on number lines.

PART–WHOLE RELATIONSHIPS

Understanding part–whole relationships is crucial to grasping the concept of cardinality. The cardinal value is the total quantity in a collection. This is sometimes called the numerosity and may be described as the 'five-ness of five'. In order to understand what a number represents, the pupil has to realize that each of the objects counted is part of the whole quantity in the collection.

Perceiving subgroups is an essential part of developing numeracy. Pupils need to see that a number contains smaller groups of numbers. This conceptual understanding is essential for efficient calculation as well so that pupils can partition numbers in ways that make them easier to use. When working with fractions pupils need to consider a quantity as a single entity which is divided into equal-sized parts.

BASE-10 RELATIONSHIPS AND PLACE VALUE

Base-10 relationships underpin the meaning of multi-digit numbers. The number system is a place value system. In a multi-digit number the value of each digit depends on its position in the number. If the place value structure is envisaged as a series of three columns, headed HTU (hundreds, tens and units), the value of each column varies by a factor of 10. Before they work with base-10 relationships, pupils need to understand the principle of exchange – that one object can represent several objects of lesser value.

It is easy to make these relationships clear by using base-10 equipment, invented by Zoltan Dienes, which provides a model of the relative size of each value. In the base-10 system, 10 ones (also called units) can be represented by 1 ten. If there are 10 tens, these can be represented by 1 hundred.

Calculation

Calculation is the act, or process, of combining or separating numbers or quantities in order to derive new information in order to solve problems. The numerical operations used to calculate are addition, subtraction, multiplication and division. Understanding how these operations are related to each makes calculation much easier. More importantly, appreciating how they are related helps to choose the most effective operation for solving a problem.

RELATIONSHIPS BETWEEN NUMERICAL OPERATIONS

Addition and subtraction are inverse operations. An inverse relationship means that the operations have the opposite effect, or that one operation reverses the effect of the other. Sometimes it is described as 'undoing' the result of the operation. For example,

3 + 2 = 5 and 5 − 3 = 2. Understanding this relationship enables pupils who find subtraction difficult to use complementary addition instead. (This method involves adding on from the smaller number and finding out how much must be added to have the same amount as the larger number.)

Multiplication and division are inverse operations. These operations are frequently taught separately, which is unfortunate as understanding one helps reinforce the other.

The inverse relationship between multiplication and division is clear if children use simple, transparent language to describe the *meaning* of the operations. For example, 3 x 4 = 12. If the child says: '3 fours make 12', it is clear that there are 3 groups with 4 items in each group. The total number of items is 12. The child who conceptualizes 3 fours will be able to solve 12 ÷ 3 by relating it to multiplication. '12 items are split into 3 groups. There will be 4 in each group.'

This kind of reasoning can be used to link each of the different conceptual models that multiplication and division represent. The area model of multiplication links directly to the long division algorithm.

Key facts

The key facts are the bonds of all the numbers to 10, and multiplication by 10. A number bond is the fixed relationship between a number and its constituent parts. Number bonds are usually learnt as two numbers which are combined to make another number. Pupils need to have automatic recall of these facts as they underpin all calculation. If pupils understand the relationship between a number and its components, they can use the information to think flexibly about numbers. For example, if they know that 3 + 4 = 7 then they can apply this information to complete the following equations: 7 − 4 = ?, 7 = 3 + ?, 4 = 7 − ?

Children should know the bonds of all the numbers to 10. Addition is commutative which means that the order in which the numbers are added does not affect the answer. Understanding this considerably reduces the number of bonds to be learned. Using the commutative property of addition means that pupils only have to learn five facts: 1 + 9, 2 + 8, 3 + 7, 4 + 6 and 5 + 5. They will then be able to derive the remaining facts of 10, which are 9 + 1, 8 + 2, 7 + 3, and 6 + 4. The doubles and near doubles bonds are 1 + 1, 1 + 2, 2 + 2, 2 + 3, 3 + 3, 3 + 4, 4 + 4, 4 + 5, 5 + 5. Provided that the child can add 1 to a number, there are then only a further six number bonds to learn. These are 4 + 2, 5 + 2, 6 + 2, 7 + 2, 8 + 2, 5 + 3 and 6 + 3.

Being able to multiply by 10 and understanding what it means is essential for working with place value and multi-digit numbers. It also helps children to quickly derive all the other multiplication facts (see page 110).

Generalizing from known facts

New facts can be derived by using knowledge of the structure of the number system and generalizing from known facts. Thus if 5 + 3 = 8, then 50 + 30 = 80, or 500 + 300 = 800.

Or 25 + 3 = 28 so 750 + 30 = 780.

Counting numbers and the measuring numbers

The counting numbers are used to enumerate quantities of discrete objects. They may also be referred to as the natural numbers. Measuring numbers are used to measure continuous quantities such as distance, time and mass. A number line shows measuring numbers which consist of both whole numbers and all the points in between them. It is easiest to understand the difference between the counting numbers and the measuring numbers by comparing a number track and a number line.

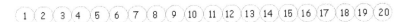

A number track has a separate, defined space for each number.
The number track does not include a position for zero.

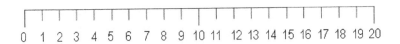

A number line shows numbers at equidistant points on the line. The
number shown at each mark, or interval, is both the point on the line,
and the distance away from the start of the line at zero. Fractions,
or parts of numbers, can also be shown on the number line.

Numerical thinking

Problem solving involves analysing information to extract what is relevant, before applying reasoning skills to reach a solution. The process of thinking about the numbers in the situation, then exploring the patterns and relationships between them to reach a logical conclusion, is called numerical thinking. Pupils also need to be able to convey their thinking to others in a variety of ways by using concrete materials, diagrams, charts and graphs as well as numerical symbols and equations.

CHAPTER 4

The Causes of Dyscalculia and Numeracy Difficulties

Everyone makes mistakes when they are learning something new. Getting things wrong is an important part of learning if it prompts you to try to figure out why something does not work and to try new ways of tackling the problem (Boaler 2009). It is important to remember this as children need time to grasp what numbers are and how the number system works. Some of the errors they make are part of normal developmental processes that are not sufficiently mature when children start school. For example, written reversals of number digits and letters may be the result of immature visuo-spatial skills, whereas reversing digits in a two-digit number indicates a lack of understanding, such as writing fourteen as 41. A child has a difficulty if the errors persist longer than expected as part of the learning process, or improves at a rate that is much slower than expected.

Teachers and parents are likely to know quite soon if a young child has difficulties. These include issues with movement, speaking and listening as well as subject-related problems such as counting accurately and remembering information. Conversely it may be difficult to spot specific difficulties more able children have as they appear to be keeping up with their peers. An indication of a specific learning difficulty is a difference in the individual's level of achievement in numeracy compared to their achievement in other subjects. The test of a learning difficulty is a distinct and unexplained gap between a person's level of expected achievement and their performance. As a rough guide, a discrepancy of 2 years or more between the expected level and the actual level may be due to a specific learning difficulty. The identification and diagnosis of specific learning difficulties is discussed in Chapter 6.

However, it is as well to remember that there are other reasons for a lack of progress and these include insufficient time allowed for the child to grasp a concept before a new one is introduced, and inappropriate teaching style for the needs of the particular child (see page 116).

Indicators of numeracy difficulties

- inability to **subitize** (recognizing up to 4 or 5 objects without counting) when the items are randomly scattered

- **counting** errors

- **miscounting** objects

- lack of **one-to-one correspondence**

- **sequencing** errors

- inability to **count backwards**

- **not understanding** the count

Examples of counting errors:

80, 90, 100, 200, 300 ('illegal count')

...48, 49, 51, 52... (decade number omitted)

...26, 27, 28, 29, 21, 22, 23... (unable to cross the decade boundary)

...70, 80, 90, 20, 21, 22... (auditory confusion between -teen and -ty endings)

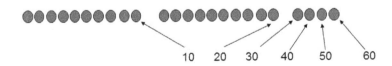

The pupil is able to recite the sequence counting in tens but uses them mechanically and does not understand what the words mean.

- **calculation** difficulties

- persistent **counting in ones** to calculate (the Counting Trap)

The counting trap: Calculate 48 ÷ 3

The child shows some understanding of the process of division but has to count out 48 by drawing circles, then crossing them out as he draws tally marks in the ovals below. Errors in either counting or recording lead to mistakes. After all the effort, the result is incorrect.

- cannot remember **number facts**

- using **unstructured** dots or tally marks to do calculations

- difficulty with **mental arithmetic**

- cannot remember **multiplication tables**

- misunderstanding maths **language** (e.g. comparative terms – more, less)

- errors **writing numbers**

- **reversing digits** in multi-digit numbers (e.g. writing thirteen as 31)

- not understanding **zero** (e.g. writing 243 as 200403)

- inaccurate **estimates**

- inability to say **roughly** how many in a group of more than 5 items *without counting*

- inability to recognize if an answer is **reasonable**

- weak **logical reasoning** skills (e.g. if 2 + 2 = 4 then 2 + 3 is one more than 2 + 2 so 2 + 3 is 5)

- inability to see **number relationships** (e.g. do not realize that if 3 + 4 = 7 then 7 − 3 = 4)

- weak at making **connections** and **transferring** knowledge (knowing that 4 + 4 = 8 therefore 14 + 4 = 18 and 80 − 40 = 40)

- problems with using **money** and telling the **time**

- lack of **place value** understanding

- errors in **formal addition and subtraction** caused by lack of place value understanding

Causes of dyscalculia and numeracy difficulties

There are many reasons why a child may have difficulty with numeracy. Sometimes it seems there is a danger that parents and professionals focus too much on what is 'wrong' with the child in their search for ways of helping them achieve the expected level of academic success. It is very important to keep a sense of perspective and remember that the purpose of identifying difficulties and their causes is to plan effective help so that the child is able to learn and ultimately take responsibility for their own learning. It is helpful to consider what causes dyscalculia and numeracy difficulties before looking at assessment in detail (see Chapters 5, 6 and 7).

Dyscalculia

A key indicator of dyscalculia is the inability to subitize. Subitizing is an ability to recognize quickly the quantity of objects in a small group of randomly scattered objects. It is an innate ability and research with very young infants has shown that they are aware of changes in the numerosity in a group. Obviously they cannot count but they can compare two groups of objects and realize if they differ in quantity.

Cognitive neuroscientists believe that developmental dyscalculia is caused by a core deficit in the structure of the brain. 'Children with dyscalculia show a core deficit in processing numerosities, which is revealed in slower and less accurate enumeration of small sets of objects and in comparing the numerosities of sets of objects or the magnitude of digits' (Butterworth and Kovas 2013, p.301).

Specific learning difficulties

Numeracy difficulties can be caused by other specific learning difficulties which may, or may not, co-occur with dyscalculia. Other cognitive weaknesses, referred to as domain general weaknesses, can also lead to difficulties learning numeracy (Simmons 2011). A range of underlying cognitive areas are involved in learning. These include working memory, language, visual reasoning and information processing. Below is a summary of some of the specific difficulties which affect both these underlying skills and numeracy skills. They may, or may not, co-occur with dyscalculia.

SPECIFIC LANGUAGE DELAY

A language delay is language development that is significantly below the norm for a child of a specified age leading to difficulty understanding language or expressing themselves.

Difficulty may affect language in general or be specifically related to mathematics.

Maths vocabulary and concepts	Slow to learn new mathematical vocabulary and difficulty using language to discuss objects and ideas which are an essential part of concept formation.

DYSLEXIA

Dyslexia is a learning difficulty that primarily affects the skills involved in accurate and fluent word reading and spelling. Characteristic features of dyslexia are difficulties in phonological awareness, verbal memory and verbal processing speed (Rose 2009).

Maths language	Slow to learn mathematical vocabulary.
Left–right orientation	Problems with directional words (left, right, up, down). Confusion with place value, number lines and formal column work.
Sequencing	Difficulty perceiving patterns in sequences causes difficulty learning to count and the days of the week and months of the year. Difficulty following arithmetical procedures.
Auditory memory	Difficulty remembering the question.
Visual memory	Difficulty developing visual images as part of concept formation. Affects the ability to remember information.
Working memory	Difficulty working with large amounts of information required for multi-stage problem solving.
Processing speed	Slow to process oral and visual information so may fail to keep up with the lesson and omit crucial information.
Visual and spatial awareness	Difficulty selecting relevant information. Difficulty finding the correct place on the page.
Conceptual ability	Difficulty grasping and retaining new information.
Reading and writing	Difficulty reading questions.

DYSPRAXIA

'Developmental dyspraxia, also known as Developmental Co-ordination Disorder (DCD), is characterized by the inability to carry out and plan sequences of coordinated movements to achieve an objective' (Kirby 2006).

Gross motor skills (control over large muscle movements)	Copying from board. Finding position on the page. Effort involved in controlling motor movement leads to lapses in concentration and results in omissions and inaccuracies copying.
Fine motor skills (control over small muscle movements).	Writing numbers. Untidy work which leads to unforced errors.
Speech difficulties	Problems articulating words. Difficulty saying multisyllabic words clearly. Difficulty saying names of multi-digit numbers. Poor auditory discrimination leading to numerical errors such as confusing endings as in thirty and thirteen.
Body image and body awareness	Finger agnosia – not knowing where the fingers are in space which causes difficulty using fingers for early counting (Dehaene 1997). Does not know how many fingers they have, despite repeated counting.
Organizational skills	Difficulty planning and organizing thoughts. Problems working in the logical, structured way required in maths
Visual perception (check that it is not a problem with eyesight)	Difficulty making sense of visual material. Frequent errors and omissions when copying information from the board or from a book.

Concentration	Pupils may fidget and wriggle because of the effort required to sit still which results in loss of concentration. Difficulty paying attention. Get tired, both mentally and physically, more quickly than peers. Hard to sit still because doing so requires conscious effort.

SENSORY PROCESSING (SOMETIMES CALLED 'SENSORY INTEGRATION')

'Sensory processing...refers to the way the nervous system receives messages from the senses and turns them into appropriate motor and behavioural responses... Sensory processing disorder (SPD) (sensory integration dysfunction) [occurs] when sensory signals don't get organized into appropriate responses' (Sensory Processing Disorder Foundation 2014).

Attention and focus	Difficulty processing the feedback from the senses leads to distraction and lack of focus on the task. Difficulty interpreting information on a 'busy' page. Difficulty concentrating when the desk is untidy.

ATTENTION DEFICIT HYPERACTIVITY DISORDER (ADHD)

ADHD is 'a heterogeneous behavioural syndrome characterized by the core symptoms of hyperactivity, impulsivity and inattention. While these symptoms tend to cluster together, some people are predominantly hyperactive and impulsive, while others are principally inattentive' (NICE 2013).

Significant attention problems	Difficulty in paying attention and easily distracted Restless and fidgety Inattention to details Makes careless mistakes Trouble finishing work or school projects Organizational problems Difficulty listening to and carrying out instructions
Overactive	Always 'on the go' Impatient
Impulsive behaviour	Act before thinking Speak before thinking by blurting out an answer Interrupting others Impulsive so difficulty in reasoning logically

General cognitive factors that affect numeracy

Academic success has become the most important factor in shaping children's lives with the result that a great deal of research is focused on ways to improve achievement as measured by formal test scores. Researchers into learning produce more and more detailed information about how children learn. They have developed ways of measuring these components of learning so that professionals can ascertain whether a particular child has developed or mastered the skills required – usually by a particular age. This also means that children who do not meet the expected levels at a particular age are identified. There are many underlying factors which affect learning and educators are increasingly expected to take these subskills, or deficits, into account when teaching. Some of the general difficulties which can affect learning numeracy are:

Anxiety is a feeling of worry, or fear, that something unpleasant is going to happen. Persistent anxiety inhibits the ability to think clearly. Anxiety may be evident from a child's demeanour and appearance:

- whispering or speaking very softly

- being reluctant to make eye contact

- bitten nails

- chewed cuffs.

Memory weakness means that the brain has significant difficulty processing information and storing it for future use. Indicators of memory weakness are:

- difficulty carrying out verbal instructions

- inability to copy accurately from a book, or from the board

- inability to rote learn information.

Visuo-spatial skills enable the brain to interpret visual information which is required in many areas for academic success. **Visuo-spatial difficulties** include problems with:

- seeing similarities and differences

- matching shapes

- recognizing objects when only part is shown

- depth perception

- imagining things which are not seen.

Language processing is the ability to understand what you hear and express what you want to say. **Language processing difficulties** may be indicated by problems such as:

- paying attention to what is said in noisy situations

- following multi-step directions, whether spoken or written

- taking part in conversations

- a limited vocabulary

- poorly structured sentences

- organizing ideas and writing them down.

Directional confusion is extreme difficulty distinguishing left from right and lack of understanding of directional words such as up, down, across, in, out. This leads to difficulty following directions. Indicators of **directional confusion** include:

- not knowing which is left or right

- difficulty following instructions

- inability to read maps or graphs

- difficulty copying movements made by someone else

- appearing disorientated

- reversing or inverting letters or numerals

- mirror writing.

Processing speed is the ability to rapidly and efficiently respond to basic stimuli. **Slow processing** hinders reading, writing and numeracy and may be indicated if the child:

- is tardy getting ready for an activity

- fails to complete assignments in a reasonable time

- daydreams

- stares into space

- appears to be lethargic

- appears to be lazy

- is slow to respond to requests.

Rhythm is a basic pre-learning skill which affects the ability to comprehend. Indicators of **lack of awareness of rhythm** include:

- inability to repeat a simple clapping sequence

- difficulty keeping in time when moving to music

- reading in a monotonous voice.

Organization is essential for efficient learning on many levels; organization of belongings, managing time, planning work, carrying out tasks. **Poor organization** impacts all areas of learning and affects daily life. Some indications of poor organization are:

- often being late

- looking dishevelled

- not having the correct books or equipment for lessons or activities

- being untidy

- inability to set out work on the page

- procrastination.

Impulsivity is the tendency to act, or react, without thinking about the consequences. **Impulsivity** is evident when children:

- rush into things

- blurt out answers

- interrupt others

- quickly become aggressive or angry.

Maths anxiety

Maths anxiety may arise when a pupil experiences repeated failure and confusion with mathematical tasks. In extreme cases, anxiety can be triggered by the word maths or other associated terms. It is a physical response which affects the pupil's ability to see and hear. Researchers at Stanford University have found that 'math anxiety was associated with reduced activity in posterior parietal and dorsolateral prefrontal cortex regions involved in mathematical reasoning'. (Young, Wu and Menon 2012, p.492). It results from frequent and prolonged exposure to a frightening situation, in this case activities associated with learning mathematics. Fear of maths arises from failure to perform at the expected level as judged by others, whether this be parents, teachers or peers. Repeated failure leads to maths anxiety; in extreme cases it may lead to maths phobia. The pupil is unable to take in or process information and may appear to 'freeze'.

Social and cultural factors

Social and cultural factors in a society also have an effect on learning numeracy. Children from poor families are more likely to start school with a limited vocabulary, which means that they start at a disadvantage because they cannot express their ideas as fluently as their more able peers. They may have difficulty understanding what is being said by teachers and so be unable to follow instructions.

This raises the question of what is expected at what age. Governments around the world produce national curriculum guidelines which specify what children are expected to know at different ages. These guidelines are based on the assumption that all children start school having developed the conceptual abilities required to learn. Unfortunately some children will be several years below their peers. This is an enormous gap when you are 5 years old and one that is likely to widen over the years, rather than close, without a great deal of intervention. There are many reasons for the gap including social problems and poverty, as well as different rates of cognitive development and learning difficulties.

There are marked differences in attitudes to maths achievement in different cultures. Some cultures believe that all pupils can achieve a reasonably high level of mathematical competence provided that they work hard. It is notable that India, China, Korea and Singapore are amongst the countries that have an expectation of mathematical competence. In many western countries there is a tacit anti-maths view. Failure in mathematics is deemed acceptable in adulthood. Parents, and some teachers, will make remarks such as: 'I was always bad at maths.' 'This is really hard.' The remark is often accompanied by a laugh. Often this is in the context of basic numeracy in the first few years of school. As a result children may receive confusing signals. The subliminal message is that maths is so hard even mum and dad find it difficult, and maths doesn't really matter. However, it also engenders the belief in the young child that failure is inevitable, rather than seeing mistakes as an opportunity to learn.

Researchers at Stanford University have found that the way pupils think about learning has a profound effect on the way that they learn and tackle problems and have coined the terms growth mindset and fixed mindset. Pupils with a growth mindset believe they can improve through their own efforts. They 'work and learn more effectively, displaying a desire for challenge and resilience in the face of failure' (Boaler 2013, p.143). Pupils with a fixed mindset are afraid of making mistakes in case it shows them to be less able than they are perceived to be.

CHAPTER 5

Assessment and Legislation

Educators need to check that students have learned knowledge and skills at the expected level for their age. All children need to get used to being assessed. Checking on how we perform has become a part of life – in the workplace as well as at school. The assessment process involves gathering, recording and interpreting information to provide evidence on which to make decisions. The results of assessment may be used to judge progress or predict performance. It is increasingly used as a means of selecting people.

Assessments need to be carried out in a timely manner and the results reported in a way that is clear and easy to read. A brief summary outlining the main findings, and suggested action, is a good way to start. Where scores are used these should be interpreted in a written summary briefly explaining what they mean, as well as any detailed explanation.

The pupil is at the heart of all assessment. Each pupil is a unique individual and this needs to be remembered in a data driven world. The main purpose of educational assessment should always be to help the pupil to learn. There is some concern about the use of labels for specific learning difficulties. Some parents find a diagnosis of a specific difficulty such as dyscalculia, attention deficit disorder (ADD) or autism helpful as it offers an explanation for the child's difficulties. However, other parents are worried that the label will be used to define the child and lead to lower expectations. Whilst this should not be the case, anecdotal reports suggest that this can sometimes happen. It is worth repeating that the individual human being should not be lost in a wealth of data, analysis and diagnosis.

Make sure that all assessments are a positive experience. Assessment has become ubiquitous in western countries. Children are assessed from the moment they are born, throughout childhood and into adulthood by a range of health and educational professionals. Adults too are continuously assessed in the workplace, both for aptitude and competence when applying for jobs and to check their progress once in work.

The range of assessments carried out can be bewildering. In schools assessment is used to judge performance and to collect data, which is used in many different ways. For example, the data may be used by governments to frame policy, by schools to hold teachers to account and to rank children, as well as for tracking progress and planning lessons. Children who have learning difficulties may also be assessed by a variety of medical professionals including behavioural optometrists, doctors, physiotherapists, psychologists and speech therapists.

Schools are required to keep test data to show how pupils are progressing. The computer has made it possible to store large quantities of data and to put this into spreadsheets which can readily compare a pupil's performance over time, as well as how well each pupil is doing in relation to their peers. This information is part of Ofsted's inspections; it is also critical for tracking the progress of pupils with specific learning difficulties. Not only does it help to show if an intervention is working, but it is also required if extra support is not working and the parents or school need to apply for funding to get specialist support.

Educational assessment falls into two broad categories: summative assessment and formative assessment. The key to navigating the assessment jungle is to ask three questions: the answers to the questions dictate the kind of assessment required to gather the information.

- Why are you doing the assessment?

- What are you going to do with the information once you have got it?

- How will you gather the information?

Educators assess pupils at the end of a period of instruction or at the end of a course to check what they have learned. This is sometimes called assessment *of* learning and a summative assessment would be used. If you are assessing to find what a pupil knows, or does not know, in order to plan what to teach, this is known as assessment *for* learning and requires formative assessment. Robert Stake summarized the difference in a memorable analogy: 'When the cook tastes the soup, that's formative assessment; when the customer tastes the soup, that's summative assessment' (Scriven 1991, p.169).

Assessment *of* learning
Why are you doing the assessment?

- To check that a pupil, or a group of pupils, has achieved a predefined level of competence.

- To rank pupils against their peers, and to track progress over time.

- To compare schools, whether in a local area, nationally or internationally in order to judge the realtive performance.

- To provide evidence on which to make decisions about educational policy at a local or national level.

What are you going to do with the information once you have got it?

The scores are recorded and used to rank pupils in a particular class, or to grade them according to agreed criteria. This information is important because it provides evidence of what a pupil knows and how they are progressing. Computers make it possible to analyse this data in many different ways and display it on charts. Scores are entered in a data base so they can be compared with results from previous tests in order to track pupil progress over time. Apart from tracking the progress of individual pupils, it can show how particular groups of children are faring, such as those with special needs, or comparing the performance of boys and girls.

Governments use the comparative data on pupil performance to hold schools and teachers to account. It has implications for funding decisions and the provision of extra help where special educational needs are involved.

The results of tests may be used to rank schools in national league tables. The implications for individual schools, as well as for teachers' jobs, depend on the pupils making progress and reaching specified levels. This has led to complaints of 'teaching to the test'.

How will you gather the information?

Assessment of learning usually involves groups of pupils taking a timed test or examination. The pupils are then ranked according to their score on the test. Most people are familiar with this form of assessment as it is used to test pupils at the end of each academic year, as well as for national examinations.

There are also tests which can be given individually, or in groups, to measure performance against pupils in other schools or countries. These are called standardized tests. They have been developed to provide benchmarks against which to measure performance. The age referenced tests measure an individual's performance against their age cohort. Norm referenced tests measure their level of competence against predefined criteria.

Assessment *for* learning

Why are you doing the assessment?

- To find out what the pupil knows and what they do not know in order to plan teaching.

- To ascertain whether a particular teaching intervention has been successful.

- To check that a pupil, or a group of pupils, have learned topics that have been taught.

- To track pupil progress over time.

What are you going to do with the information once you have got it?

The information is used to plan what to teach and how to teach it. However, it is useful to record test scores to measure how a pupil improves (or not) over time, both for the pupil's sake and to check that teaching is having the desired effect. Detailed suggestions for how to record information to plan teaching are given in Chapter 6.

Not everything that is assessed can be measured. Educators also need to gather qualitative, or descriptive, data. It includes finding out about how pupils think about numbers and what strategies they use to apply their knowledge. Assessment for learning also looks at pupils' learning skills, the strengths and weaknesses they may have in memory or visuo-spatial skills and their attitude to learning in general.

How will you gather the information?

Assessment for learning involves diagnostic assessment. The scripts from written tests can provide a great deal of information about the way that a pupil thinks about numbers and what they do, or do not, understand. More important is formative assessment which involves observations and discussions.

Numeracy is a hierarchical subject so it is relatively easy to divide topics into the subskills required and find out whether pupils understand numbers and can use them to solve problems. Pupils are encouraged to talk about what they are doing and thinking as they tackle tasks. Formative assessment provides real-time feedback, which helps pupils develop reasoning skills as well as enabling the teacher or therapist to adjust what and how they are intervening.

National and international assessment

High-stakes tests and low-stakes tests

Children, parents and teachers often worry about tests because of the impact that the results have on their lives. Some tests are more important than others: it depends how the results are going to be used. Assessing can be divided into high-stakes testing and low-stakes testing. Major life choices often depend on high-stakes tests such as school or university examinations, or aptitude tests for jobs. Low-stakes tests are those that provide information that does not have such a dramatic impact on the course of a person's life, such as end-of-year school exams and assessments for planning teaching and learning.

Universities use the results of examinations and tests as part of the selection data for admissions decisions. Employers use grades from both school and university examinations and assessments as part of the employment selection process. Increasingly, job applicants have to pass online tests in verbal and non-verbal reasoning before they can even get an application form.

The data from standardized tests is important for government policy makers. It is used as evidence on which to make changes to the curriculum and the way that schools teach it.

Programme for International Student Assessment (PISA) tests

PISA tests matter because governments take their findings very seriously and they affect educational policy decisions. PISA is part of the Organisation for Economic Co-operation and Development (OECD) which is an international organization which aims 'to promote policies that will improve the economic and social well-being of people around the world'.

> PISA is unique because it develops tests which are not directly linked to the school curriculum. The tests are designed to assess to what extent students at the end of compulsory education, can apply their knowledge to real-life situations and be equipped for full participation in society. The information collected through background questionnaires also provides context which can help analysts interpret the results.
>
> (OECD n.d.)

The PISA tests take place every three years. This international survey tests 15-year-old pupils in reading, mathematics and science. The results are used to rank the educational performance of economies.

Usually this will mean whole countries, but in the case of China individual cities take part, not the whole country, hence the use of 'economies' rather than 'countries'. Pupils in 65 economies took part in the PISA tests that took place in 2012. The focus was on mathematics. A sample of 510,000 pupils represented 28 million pupils in the age cohort.

The results from PISA tests enable governments to compare pupils' performance over time and assess the impact of their education policies. The results are also used to compile an international league table of countries' educational performance. In recent PISA surveys pupils in western economies have performed relatively poorly compared to those in many Asian economies. This has led to curriculum changes in many countries, including the US and the UK.

Assessment in schools in the UK

In the UK data on pupil progress is required by law. Pupil progress is assessed at regular intervals throughout their schooling. The education systems are slightly different in the four countries that make up the UK. At present compulsory schooling ends at the age of 16.

Pupils who continue education after the age of 16 may either study for vocational qualifications, which emphasize the practical element, or choose the academic route. In Scotland the Curriculum for Excellence defines five levels of attainment during the years of compulsory schooling. Each level is reached based on the teacher's assessment of a student's abilities and readiness to progress. Assessment includes standardized exams which the pupil sits when the teacher decides the pupils is ready to do so. Pupils who continue academic education after age 16 study for Higher and Advanced Higher qualifications.

In England and Wales, pupils are assessed when they start school in Reception and at the end of their first year, in National Curriculum tests (often referred to as SATs) at the ages of 7, 11 and 14 and at the end of compulsory schooling at the age of 16. A variety of academic qualifications are available after that age: Advanced-levels (A-levels), the Baccalaureate and the Pre-U. The Northern Ireland Curriculum is similar to that of England and Wales. The information below is an overview of the assessment process in England and Wales.

EARLY YEARS FOUNDATION STAGE (EYFS)

The Early Years Foundation Stage (EYFS) sets standards for the learning, development and care of children from birth to 5 years old.

PRIMARY SCHOOL

Primary school children are assessed shortly after they start Reception class at around the age of 4. This baseline assessment is to find out how ready the child is for school. No writing is required; it is an oral assessment which the teacher should conduct in a relaxed and friendly way.

There is a statutory assessment at the end of Reception. In the numeracy part of the test children are asked if they can recognize written numbers and to count small toys, amongst other tasks. Children are also tested for vocabulary skills and cognitive skills. It is an oral assessment. The results are collated to provide a threshold score. If the child fails to meet the threshold score, extra funding is available so that extra help can start immediately. The funding lasts throughout the child's primary schooling.

Children mature at different rates and some teachers are concerned that these very young children might be labelled as having a difficulty when this is not the case. It is not possible to diagnose specific learning difficulties such as dyslexia and dyscalculia at this young age. The point of the test is to quickly pick up on any early warning signs of potential difficulties and intervene as soon as possible. It is not necessary to label the child but it is essential to do something to help before they become anxious, develop the attitude 'I'm different. I can't do it' and possibly develop behavioural problems to mask their failure.

Statutory Assessment Tests (SATS)

Statutory Assessment Tests (SATS) are developed by the Standards and Testing Agency (STA), which is an executive agency of the Department for Education. The content of the tests is regulated by the Office of Qualifications and Examination Regulation (Ofqual).

The tests take place at the end of Year 2 for Key Stage 1 (KS1), at the end of Year 6 for Key Stage 2 (KS2) and at the end of Year 9 for Key Stage 3 (KS3). (In Northern Ireland this equates to Year 10.)

Key Stage 1 (KS1) SAT test

The KS1 assessment is a written test at the end of Year 2. The results of these tests are very important as they indicate whether a child has learned the knowledge and skills expected for their age. If they have not, it is a trigger for additional support.

The test results are also very important for the school. The KS1 tests are standardized so they show how a child is progressing compared with children around the country. They are used as the benchmark against which to judge the school's effectiveness over time. The results from the KS2 tests four years later are compared with the KS1 results to check that pupils have made expected progress.

Key Stage 2 (KS2) SAT test

The KS2 assessment is a written test at the end of Year 6. Children are expected to achieve a level 4 or above. The results of these tests are very important for the children because they give the secondary schools information about what the pupils know, or don't know. This is essential for planning what help may be required.

The results are important for the schools because they are used to rank schools in the UK in national league tables. Parents use this information when choosing schools. The KS2 results are also used to hold governors, head teachers and teachers to account by the local authority and by Ofsted.

SECONDARY SCHOOL
Key Stage 3 (KS3) SAT tests

At 14 years old pupils take the KS3 tests in English, mathematics and science. These are externally set and marked. They are also assessed by their teachers against the attainment targets in the curriculum subjects at this level – English, mathematics, science, history, geography, design and technology, information and communication technology, modern foreign languages, citizenship, art and design, music and physical education.

Key Stage 4 (KS4)
GCSE (General Certificate of Secondary
Education) and vocational qualifications

Compulsory education ends at the age of 16 in the UK. Pupils either take the GCSE exams in individual curriculum subjects or they can take vocational qualifications. Pupils with difficulties who are working below this level can take Entry Level qualifications.

INTERNAL ASSESSMENT BY SCHOOLS

In the past there was a national assessment framework in the UK which schools could use to track progress through the primary years. This has been abolished and schools are now free to draw up their own assessment frameworks. In practice this means that schools may collaborate to produce assessment tools, local authorities may be involved or private organizations will publish materials that schools can use.

Before September 2014 the tests were graded into 'levels'. These have been abolished and replaced by 'descriptors' which outline what pupils are expected to know by a particular age. Various terms are used to express this idea because of sensitivities around labelling children. They indicate *below* expected level, *at* expected level, *above* expected level.

EDUCATION AFTER AGE 16

Vocational qualifications are practical qualifications that prepare students for jobs. There are many different kinds and they are run by a variety of organizations including particular industries or companies, professional bodies and tertiary colleges. The assessment of vocational qualifications may be done in a number of different ways, such as tests and examinations, observation, projects or a portfolio of evidence. In some cases vocational qualifications may be accepted for entry to university.

Students who continue with an academic education study courses that are assessed by examinations. Coursework may form part of the assessment. There are a variety of higher level academic qualifications offered in the UK. These include A-level (General Certificate of Education Advanced Level), the Pre-U (Pre University) and the ICB (International Baccalaureate). Scotland, Ireland and Wales also offer alternative higher level school leaving certificates.

Applications and admissions to universities and higher education (HE) institutions in the UK are managed by UCAS (Universities and Colleges Admissions System). It produces a tariff system which enables the level of different qualifications to be compared. Major changes are being implemented in 2017 in order to clarify and simplify the system.

Assessment in schools in the US

In the US education is organized on a federal basis. Congress passed laws that mean that schools that receive state funding must assess the progress of all students in basic skills at selected grade levels. Originally called the Elementary and Secondary Education Act of 1965, it has been periodically updated and in 2001 the name was changed to the No Child Left Behind Act of 2001 (NCLB). Because each state develops its own assessments, it is not possible to compare standards between states.

Comparative national standards are measured by the National Association of Educational Progress (NAEP) which is run by the National Center of Educational Statistics (NCES) at the Department of Education. NAEP measures the progress of students across the US by testing representative samples of students in Grades 4, 8 and 12 every year. The results are used to monitor and compare the progress of students in different states in order to plan improved teaching. Every four years there is an assessment of pupils aged 9, 13 and 17 in mathematics and reading to monitor long-term trends.

In 2009 a nationwide effort started to develop Common Core State Standards (CCSS). The initiative involved 48 states and was led by the National Governors Association Center for Best Practices (NGA) and the Council of Chief State School Officers (CCSSO). A very wide range of educators, parents and state leaders took part. The resulting Common Core Standards provide frameworks which 'provide clear and consistent learning goals to help prepare students for college, career, and life. The standards clearly demonstrate what students are expected to learn at each grade level, so that every parent and teacher can understand and support their learning' (NGA 2010).

In the Common Care Standards for Mathematics, the key changes involve focus, coherence and rigour:

> The Common Care calls for greater focus in mathematics. Rather than racing to cover many topics in a mile-wide, inch-deep curriculum, the standards ask math teachers to significantly narrow and deepen the way time and energy are spent in the classroom... Coherence [in] linking topics and thinking across grades...[and] Rigor [in pursuing] conceptual understanding, procedural skills and fluency, and application with equal intensity.
>
> (NGA 2010)

HIGH SCHOOL ACHIEVEMENT AND COLLEGE ENTRY ASSESSMENT

The most important assessments for many students are the standardized tests used to measure high school achievement and required for entry to colleges and universities in America. They are designed to measure preparedness for college and academic potential. These test scores are one of the factors that admissions officers take into account because they enable comparison between students from different educational systems, both within America and internationally.

The two most widely used tests are the SAT and the ACT. Both tests are referred to by naming the letters in the names. The SAT is an abbreviation of the Scholastic Aptitude Test which is run by the College Board. The ACT derives its name from the company that started it, American College Testing (now called ACT Incorporated). The College Board and ACT Inc. are independent educational organizations which undertake research and provide training and advice, as well as managing a range of educational programmes. The College Board also provides and monitors Advanced Placement (AP) programmes which offer a college-level curriculum and examinations for high school students. AP scores may also be taken into account by college admissions officers.

Special educational needs provision in the UK

In the UK the rights of pupils with special educational needs are covered by law. The main legal framework in Scotland is The Education (Additional Support for Learning) (Scotland) Act 2004, amended in 2009. Changes to education law proposed in the Education (Scotland) Bill 2015 are designed to clarify the rights of pupils with special needs.

The relevant law in Northern Ireland is the Special Educational Needs and Disability (Northern Ireland) Order 2005 which enacted amendments to the existing Education (Northern Ireland) Order 1996.

Major changes to educational policy in England and Wales were introduced in September 2014. The changes affect what is taught and how teaching is assessed. There have been changes regarding the provision made for pupils with numeracy difficulties and who is responsible for providing it.

The Children and Families Act 2014

The Children and Families Act 2014 was intended to simplify the education process. Schools have greater freedom to teach what the children in their care need to know. The Act covers the education, health and social care of young people from birth to 25 years old. Health and social care issues affect learning. Therefore it is important that educational, medical and social professionals work together to help the child or young person. Local authorities have to provide a Local Offer which explains what help is available in the area and how to get it. It should not be simply a directory of existing services.

The views of parents and young people are at the heart of the reforms; however, this comes with greater responsibility for them to take an active role. Classroom teachers have always had responsibility for managing the needs of the children in their care. 'Quality first' teaching is a feature of the new legislation. Class teaching is expected to be more inclusive and meet the needs of all the children in the class. The aim is to reduce the need for SEN interventions outside the classroom.

Special educational needs and disabilities (SEND)

The new SEND regulations place the onus on teachers to address any learning difficulties in the classroom. If the difficulties persist, then there is a graduated approach: extra tuition takes place in small groups, and if the child still fails to make progress they are offered one-to-one support. All the help that is offered must be documented and progress tracked. 'Teachers are **responsible** and **accountable** for the progress and development of the pupils in their class, including where pupils access support from teaching assistants or specialist staff' (Department for Education and Department for Health 2005, p.99).

The Act introduces the biggest changes to SEND provision in 30 years. The aim is to simplify the process and make it easier for families to get the help they need. In school, the classroom teacher is the person with whom to discuss any concerns. Classroom teachers monitor the progress of each child. If the child has persistent difficulty with the work they are asked to do, this is called a 'cause for concern'. Discussion with the head teacher and the SENCO (Special Educational Needs Coordinator) may lead to extra help which is called SEN Support.

There is a graduated approach to SEN Support consisting of three stages. In the new Code of Practice the stages called Wave 1, Wave 2 and Wave 3 have been renamed Universal, Targeted and Personalised interventions. What the child needs to learn, who will help them and how often needs to be clearly set out. A system called SMART targets is often used to make sure that the teaching is focused. (SMART stands for specific, measurable, achievable, realistic and timed.) An example would be to learn the bonds of 10 within 10 weeks. Children and their parents are involved in setting the targets.

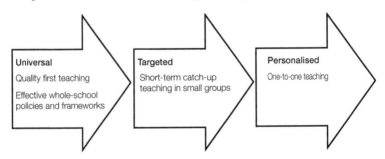

Universal
Quality first teaching
Effective whole-school policies and frameworks

Targeted
Short-term catch-up teaching in small groups

Personalised
One-to-one teaching

Universal (Wave 1): The teacher is expected to address any difficulties in the classroom with the help of a teaching assistant (TA).

Targeted (Wave 2): If the difficulties persist, then extra tuition takes place in small groups taught by a TA or specialist staff. The teacher is still responsible for what is taught.

Personalised (Wave 3): If there is insufficient progress after one term (about 10 weeks), the pupil is given individual teaching. This is likely to be for children who are working well below the expected level.

Education, Health and Care Plan (EHCP)

The Education, Health and Care Plan (EHCP) is designed to simplify the process for helping children or young people with SEND. It integrates the child's needs – health, social and educational. The family is at the heart of the EHCP which means that parents or carers have to take part in discussions with the professionals involved with their child. They work together to 'co-produce' a plan to support the child.

EHCP replaced the Statement of Special Needs in the UK in September 2014. (Pupils who already have a SEN Statement will continue to have that support. A change to EHCP will be made gradually for those children.)

The EHCP sets out what help the child will get and who will provide it. The process for assessment under the new law is more rigorous and complex than it was previously because a substantial amount of documentary evidence is required. This includes data from the school about the child's progress and discussions with parents, as well as reports and information from social care and health professionals. Once all the documentation is in place, parents meet the local authority coordinator to formulate a plan. The Local Authority looks at all the evidence and decides whether or not to issue an EHCP. The EHCP is protected by law. Once an EHCP has been issued, the education provision has to be provided. The parents or young person have the right to appeal to the Special Educational Needs and Disability Tribunal if the EHCP is turned down by the Local Authority, or if they are not happy with the amount of support provided.

Meetings with parents

SEND SUPPORT

Parents are expected to be actively involved with their children's SEND teaching. The teacher, with support from the SENCO, meets with the parents of children with SEND at least three times a year. These meetings will be longer than most parent–teacher meetings and will review the issues and plan what to do. The term used in the SEN Code of Practice is 'co-production' which emphasizes that the parent and child have to be involved in the decisions.

EHCP

Parents work closely with the classroom teacher and SENCO to prepare the evidence for the application for an EHCP. They will also meet any other professionals involved in their child's care.

Special educational needs provision in the US

The rights of pupils with disabilities and their parents are covered by the Individuals with Disabilities Education Act (IDEA). This federal law was first passed in 1975 and has been amended since then. It is currently known as IDEA 2004. The aim of the law was to protect the rights of children with disabilities and give their parents a voice in their child's education. This law guarantees the right to a *free and appropriate public education* (FAPE) for children and young people with disabilities, including specific learning disabilities. The word 'appropriate' is important as it means that the education must meet the individual's needs. However, it is important to realize that this does not mean that a pupil with disabilities has a right to preferential treatment. Nor does it mean that a pupil with disabilities automatically qualifies for special education services (Lee 2014).

IDEA (2004) sets out, in detail, the process and criteria for accessing services for children from infancy to the end of high school education, or age 21, whichever comes first.

Identification

The school has a legal duty to identify and evaluate all pupils who need special educational provision. This passage in the IDEA 2004 is referred to as Child Find. It states: 'All children with disabilities… regardless of the severity of their disabilities, and who are in need of special education and related services, are identified, located and evaluated' (Section 612(a)(3) of IDEA).

Evaluation

If the school suspects that a pupil has a disability, it is required to conduct an evaluation. Parents may also request an evaluation. The parent's written consent is required before an evaluation can take place. A thorough evaluation may involve a range of relevant professionals from both within and outside the school. If the parents are not satisfied with the evaluation, they may request an independent educational evaluation.

Once it is agreed that the pupil is eligible for specialist support, the next step is to draw up an IEP.

IEP

An IEP (Individual Education Plan) is a document which spells out the disabilities that the pupil has, and what educational services and support need to be provided. It sets specific educational goals and the time by which those goals should be met. Wherever possible the support should be in the least restrictive environment in a community school. If this is not possible, the IEP sets out where the teaching will take place.

An IEP is drawn up at a meeting between the parents and all the professionals involved with the child such as speech therapists, educational psychologists and occupational therapists. This might include specialists from outside the school as well as the classroom teacher and other school staff. The parents must be given written notice of the meeting.

Parents must give informed consent to the IEP. Informed consent means that you understand what is being proposed. The IDEA law stipulates that all information must be clear and anything you do not understand explained fully. If parents disagree with the proposed IEP, there are procedures in place to safeguard their rights so they can go to mediation and, ultimately, the law to enforce those rights.

Provision

The school has a legal duty to ensure that the services and support set out in the IEP are provided.

The school needs to monitor the pupil's progress regularly and keep records. The IEP sets out how the progress will be checked. Written reports on the pupil's progress will be sent to the parents as agreed in the IEP.

Review

The IEP is reviewed annually at a meeting of all the professionals, to which the parents are invited. IDEA states that pupils should be re-evaluated every three years to see if they still require support. However, the parents and school may agree that this is not necessary.

SAT and ACT accommodations

Students who have documented learning difficulties may be eligible for accommodations, such as extra time or a reader, for the SAT and the ACT tests. It is essential for the student to apply directly to the College Board or ACT Incorporated in good time for consideration for these accommodations.

CHAPTER 6

Identifying and Diagnosing Dyscalculia and Numeracy Difficulties

Dyscalculia screening tests

There is a difference between identifying dyscalculia and finding the specific area of numerical difficulty. As discussed in Chapter 4, there are many reasons for failing to learn basic numeracy. There are two computer-based tests which are designed to establish whether the cause of the difficulty may be dyscalculia. It should be noted that these tests are an indication of dyscalculia; they do not constitute a diagnosis of dyscalculia. Diagnosis requires extensive investigation by a chartered psychologist.

Dyscalculia Screener

The Dyscalculia Screener is designed to distinguish the dyscalculic learner from other low-attaining learners. It is an online screener which was developed by Brian Butterworth at University College London (UCL). The Dyscalculia Screener tests four areas of number ability:

- simple reaction time

- dot enumeration

- number comparison

- arithmetic achievement.

The test investigates the pupil's numerical potential in a way that is independent of other cognitive skills such as reading or language. It measures how quickly the pupil responds to a series of tasks. The tasks include identifying how many dots there are in a collection, comparing the size of numbers and simple addition and multiplication. Both accuracy and response times are taken into account.

The results indicate whether the pupil may have dyscalculia. The results are displayed in a bar chart, and a succinct report explains what the scores mean and suggests what further assessment or intervention should be undertaken. The scores are standardized so that the pupil's attainment level can be compared with the national average.

DysCalculiUM

DysCalculiUM is an online screening test for adults and pupils over the age of 16. It is a comprehensive assessment of basic number concepts, the application of numbers to everyday situations, as well as covering key cognitive areas including conceptual, visuo-spatial, directional and inferential abilities.

The report at the end of the test gives a profile of each person's abilities and difficulties and identifies problem areas.

Diagnostic assessment

Carry out a diagnostic assessment to establish the pupil's attitude to learning and to maths and to produce evidence from which to plan effective teaching. The aim is to establish the pupil's level of competence and confidence as well as finding the areas of weakness and misunderstanding. It is important to make contemporaneous notes as unobtrusively as possible.

Diagnostic assessment requires both analysis of written work and observation of the pupil's approach to numbers. The assessor can glean information by analysing the errors made in written tests and those arising in other written work. However, the essential element of diagnostic, or formative, assessment is careful observation of, and discussion with, the pupil. Be aware of signs of tension and anxiety.

Create as relaxed an atmosphere as possible. Much information about a pupil's attitude to education and their verbal ability can be gathered by starting with a general chat about their family, hobbies and interests. Ask what they feel about maths and what they like as well as what they find difficult. Then investigate key areas of numeracy starting with counting and basic calculation to discover what the pupil knows, what they do not know and how they think about numbers. Look for evidence of logical reasoning and strategies. Stop when the pupil has made about three errors. The aim is to establish the pupil's level of competence; teaching will start from this point

There is a wide variety of published diagnostic assessments. It is not possible to review all the assessments available so a few are given as examples. The ones mentioned here can be used without any specialist training.

Sandwell Early Numeracy Test

This test explores five strands of basic number skills: identification, oral counting, value, object counting and language. It is an oral test so needs to be administered on a one-to-one basis. The findings can be used to draw up targeted teaching programmes and to provide evidence for SEN interventions.

The results give a standardized age-related score. It is designed to assess children from ages 4 to 8. It is widely used in the UK to provide a baseline assessment when a child starts school and to measure their progress at the end of Reception, and can also be used for older pupils who are struggling in order to identify particular numerical weaknesses, and to analyse skills and to monitor progress.

More Trouble with Maths

This book (Chinn 2012) provides a range of assessments for the underlying learning skills required and written tests of numerical knowledge and skills. The tests are standardized so give an indication of how the pupil is faring compared with their age group. The author explains how to interpret the information to identify the barrier to learning and plan suitable teaching at the appropriate level.

The Dyscalculia Assessment

This book (Emerson and Babtie 2013) is a diagnostic tool to gather information about a pupil's sense of number in order to plan suitable intervention at the appropriate level. The assessment answers the questions:

- What does the pupil know, or not know?

- How does the pupil think about numbers?

- Where do the difficulties lie, and what causes them?

- How do you draw up a teaching plan to solve the problem?

No special training is required to use The Dyscalculia Assessment; it can be used by parents and teaching assistants (TAs), as well as teachers and SEN specialists. Detailed guidance explains how to investigate each stage of learning to count and to calculate in order to find out where understanding has broken down.

The assessment is not timed and does not give test scores so it is not standardized. It is not necessary to carry out the entire assessment; the aim is to find the point at which to begin teaching. Assessment can stop and teaching begin once this starting point is established.

Diagnosis of dyscalculia or other specific learning difficulties

A formal diagnosis of dyscalculia can only be made by a chartered psychologist who may be either an educational psychologist or a clinical psychologist. There are several reasons for getting a formal diagnosis of a specific learning difficulty:

- to investigate the cognitive profile of a child in order to provide suitable help

- to provide evidence for the need for extra support at school

- to establish what specific help is required

- to be allowed extra time to complete work in examinations

- to be allowed help from a reader or an amanuensis in examinations

- to access a wide range of support at university.

There appears to be a move to change the emphasis from diagnosing individual specific learning difficulties (including dyscalculia, dyslexia, attention deficit disorder) to a broader, more general category called specific learning difficulties. Problems in particular academic areas would be noted. In this view the particular difficulty is seen as a symptom of more general problems that affect learning. This approach has grown out of research findings that suggest there is a great deal of co-occurrence between specific learning difficulties. Numeracy difficulties may be caused by a variety of conditions and difficulties as discussed in Chapter 4.

A variety of standardized tests is available to measure a person's cognitive profile, investigating both verbal ability and performance. These are often referred to as IQ (intelligence quotient) tests. Intelligence tests have a useful role to play in providing information about cognitive functioning. The profiles can be used to diagnose specific learning difficulties. This information is used to determine the best way to help the pupil.

In the past, people believed that intelligence was fixed at birth and could be measured by scoring people's ability to do a variety of tasks. The results were used to predict academic ability. This had consequences for people's expectations of children's potential. In some cases children with a high IQ felt unduly pressurized to succeed, while little was expected of those with low IQs. This could become a self-fulfilling prophecy and lead to lack of motivation. The psychologist Reuven Feuerstein challenged the notion of a fixed IQ and showed that thinking skills can be improved with a resultant improvement in IQ scores. Recent advances in educational neuroscience indicate that the brain is much more malleable than originally thought. It is becoming less common to specify a particular IQ score; instead the results are given in a range with descriptors indicating whether the results are average or higher or lower than average.

Wechsler Intelligence Scales for Children (WISC-V)

The WISC is probably the most widely used intelligence test. It is revised periodically and the WISC-V is the latest version. Cognitive ability is assessed in verbal comprehension, perceptual reasoning, working memory and processing speed by using subtests in each of these areas. The scores from the subtests are used to formulate an index of scores for each factor. This information highlights learning strengths and weaknesses, and indicates the kind of teaching style that will be most successful.

VERBAL COMPREHENSION INDEX

This investigates the pupil's understanding of, and use of, oral language. It also checks the ability to reason. The results give an indication of educational potential and may predict academic success because language is such an essential part of learning.

Verbal comprehension and reasoning ability are important for understanding mathematical concepts and developing new ones.

PERCEPTUAL REASONING INDEX

Timed tests are used to investigate visuo-spatial and perceptual skills. Logical reasoning is required to do well in these tasks, which involve manipulating objects, completing patterns and identifying common properties in pictures.

Understanding pattern lies at the heart of all mathematics. Difficulty analysing patterns impacts numeracy, where pupils need to understand the relationships between numbers as well as work with shapes.

WORKING MEMORY

The subtests measure auditory short-term memory, sequencing skills, attention and concentration, visuo-spatial imaging and processing speed as well as numerical reasoning.

Working memory is a crucial factor in learning mathematics. Calculations require children to hold information in working memory while they retrieve known facts from long-term memory to use to derive new information.

PROCESSING SPEED

The subtests designed to measure processing speed include measures of short-term memory, learning ability, visual perception, visuo-motor coordination, cognitive flexibility, attention and motivation as well as auditory comprehension, perceptual organization and planning and learning ability.

Visualization plays an essential role in understanding numerical concepts. A weakness in the subskills in this area will lead to significant difficulty in learning basic numeracy if the pupil is not allowed to work at their own pace.

Assessment and diagnosis of other difficulties that affect learning numeracy

It will be clear from the list of cognitive processes that are investigated by the WISC-V that there are many factors that contribute to difficulty in learning numeracy. Other areas that might require assessment are motor skills, perception including visual perceptual skills and auditory skills, and speech and language. In-depth assessment of these areas would be carried out by professionals including occupational therapists, behavioural optometrists or speech and language therapists.

Motor skills

Motor skills are essential for understanding and adjusting to the world. The ability to control the body has an impact on developing spatial and directional understanding which affects learning and thinking. It takes a long time for children to develop efficient motor skills. Proficiency in any particular skill should be related to what is expected of a child at a particular age. Sometimes people try to speed up what is a normal rate of development; this may lead to anxiety which in turn can lead to behavioural problems.

Perception

One of the basic aspects of an individual's ability to think and know (cognition) is how one is able to perceive certain stimuli. Assessing perception skills – observing how individuals may respond to things they see, hear, and touch – is, therefore, a basic part of assessing cognitive function.

(Encyclopedia of Children's Health)

It is not enough to know whether a child can see, hear and touch; you need to know how they interpret what they see, hear and touch and what conclusions they draw from this information. Merely asking a child to copy a simple shape, or to tell you what they see, can be helpful. Sometimes it elicits some surprising information.

Visual perception is crucial for learning. Visual perception enables you to *make sense* of what you see. This is different to visual acuity which is the clarity of an image. There is a high correlation between visual perceptual difficulties and mathematical difficulties.

Auditory perception is the ability to comprehend and interpret auditory signals. The skills required for auditory perception include auditory discrimination, auditory memory, auditory blending and auditory comprehension:

- auditory discrimination: the ability to differentiate among phonemes – the smallest significant units of sound in a language

- auditory memory: the ability to recall a sequence of auditory sounds

- auditory blending: the ability to perceive separate phonemes, divide a word into phonemes and combine phonemes into words

- auditory comprehension: the ability to comprehend and interpret information that is presented orally.

Speech and language

Poor verbal abilities have a significant effect on learning so it is essential to identify any difficulties as early as possible and provide suitable intervention. Delayed speech and language and restricted vocabulary, for the child's age, may be indicators of problems in this area. Assessment needs to be carried out by a speech and language therapist.

There can be many reasons for language delay including specific language delay, receptive and expressive language difficulties, social factors, deafness or autism spectrum disorders.

PART 2

Teaching

Effective teaching starts with a clear plan based on evidence obtained from diagnostic assessment.

Assess the pupil to find out what the pupil can do, what they do not know, and how they think about numbers. Use a diagnostic assessment and summarize the findings to provide a Summary Numeracy Profile (*The Dyscalculia Assessment* is a detailed guide to conducting a diagnostic assessment and interpreting the results) (Emerson and Babtie 2013). This information will help establish what the pupil needs to learn. Teaching will start from the point at which the pupil is secure; this is just before the point at which their understanding has broken down.

Set clear **goals** to be achieved within a realistic time frame. The **long-term goal** may either be particular subject matter, or aligned with curriculum expectations.

The **medium-term plan** outlines the concepts and knowledge to be taught in a specified time and gives the criteria for checking that the goal has been achieved.

Each **individual lesson plan** focuses on one concept and the associated knowledge. Teach each concept using **multi-sensory methods**. Check that the pupil **understands** the concept before moving on to a new area.

CHAPTER 7

Planning and Assessment for Teaching

Assessment is part of the teaching process. As discussed in the previous chapter, numerical difficulties will be evident from the pupil's work in class and the results of class tests and examinations. It may be possible to analyse these errors to find the source of the pupil's difficulty; however, it is advisable to carry out a thorough diagnostic investigation of how the child thinks about numbers as well as finding out what they can and cannot do.

There is often a great deal of information about a child available by the time they are referred for additional teaching. It can be helpful to assess the child *before* reading all the related information in order to avoid prejudging the child and their performance. Teaching needs to take into account the findings from other professionals, as well as information from teachers and parents; however, this can be summarized and incorporated later.

Diagnostic assessment involves gathering general information from the child about their attitudes and interests as well as specific information about their numerical knowledge, skills and approach to learning. Assessors can glean much information about the pupil's problem solving behaviour if the investigation is carried out as an ongoing conversation. This is also important to ascertain what mathematical vocabulary pupils can use to express their ideas. The aim of the assessment is to find the point at which to start teaching. This means identifying the point at which understanding has broken down. Teaching can start once this has been established. Experience has shown that pupils with dyscalculia or numeracy difficulties lack understanding of basic numerical concepts. For that reason it is not necessary to investigate their knowledge of fractions and decimals as these depend on sound foundations with whole numbers.

Assessment of basic numeracy should cover the following broad areas:

- number sense and counting – subitizing, estimation, counting, sequencing, reading and writing numbers

- basic calculation – addition and subtraction, key facts, and logical reasoning

- place value – the principle of exchange, the concept of place value, flexibility in calculation methods and the application of prior knowledge to derive new facts

- multiplication and division – the concepts as well as knowledge of the multiplication tables

- word problems – establishing what a question is asking and identifying the appropriate numerical operation to solve the problem

- formal written numeracy – using formal written algorithms, the step-by-step procedures to do calculations involving multi-digit numbers; this requires understanding of the principle of exchange.

Use a structured set of questions and activities with sufficient space to note responses. In some circumstances it may be appropriate to use a sound recorder. Teachers may devise their own assessment schedule but it saves time to use one that is already available. There are a wide variety of diagnostic assessment tools. The guidelines given below are based on *The Dyscalculia Assessment* (Emerson and Babtie 2013), which is a manual developed at Emerson House in London and written for use by parents and non-specialists as well as for SENCOs, teachers and teaching assistants.

Carrying out the assessment

It is very important to carry out assessments in a friendly, encouraging manner so that the pupil is as relaxed as possible. Speak clearly and give short clear instructions and questions and allow the pupil plenty of time to respond. Make sure that the space used for the assessment is clear of clutter, in order to avoid distractions and engender a sense of calm. Any equipment required should be ready before the session starts and kept on a low table, or a chair out of the line of sight. Materials used in the outline below include a small beanbag, paper and pencil, counters, dice, and reward stickers for young children.

Start with a short chat and a few introductory activities to help the child to relax. The length of an assessment session varies according to the ability and perseverance of the child. If a child cannot do a task, or becomes distressed, the assessor should move on to the next task or stop the test. The point of assessment is to find out what pupils know, and where understanding has broken down, so it is unhelpful to force the child to continue once they are failing. Diagnostic assessment for teaching should not be timed in order to avoid the stress that may arise from worrying about time pressure affecting the pupil's performance.

Initial chat

Allow about 5 minutes for the initial discussion. Ask the pupil about their feelings about school, and what hobbies and interests they may have. Asking them to write their name and date of birth may provide information on fine motor skills, and whether they need to have their face very close to the page, a possible indicator of visual perceptual issues. Sometimes children do not know their date of birth, which may indicate memory weakness or lack of awareness of numbers in the real world.

Look at the whole child while you are chatting. Their demeanour, state of dress and general attitude can be revealing. Chewed nails or clothing may indicate anxiety. Fiddling with hair and rocking on a chair may be caused by attentional problems, or may indicate visual or developmental issues. Dishevelled clothing may be the result of disorganization or dyspraxic tendencies.

A few physical activities can help the child to relax. Most children enjoy the following activities if they are introduced in a light-hearted way. They are not an assessment of the underlying visual perceptual skills, spatial skills, and so on, but they can provide useful information about these areas.

Give the child the following tasks and allow plenty of time for them to respond. Tell them to wait until you finish speaking before they move. Do not comment on any errors; simply move on to the next activity.

Wave your left hand.

Can they respond quickly or are they unsure which their left hand is? Ask them to put their hands at their sides.

Put your right hand on your head. Put your left hand on your left knee.

Children with difficulties frequently find it difficult to carry out this instruction. Some children ask for the question to be repeated, which indicates that they may find it difficult to process verbal information. This has important implications for learning numeracy.

Asking a child to throw and catch a small bean bag provides information about their coordination, and eye movement – whether they can track the path to throw it accurately, and their eyes converge to watch the bag as they catch it.

Number sense and counting

Check whether the child has a feel for the size of quantities, is able to count orally and can read and write numbers. Start by investigating quantities to 10. If the child is successful, then move on to larger numbers.

SUBITIZING, ESTIMATING AND COUNTING OBJECTS

Scatter a few counters (4 or less) and ask the pupil: *How many are there?*

The child should be able to respond quickly without having to count the objects. If they are unable to do this, it indicates that they may be dyscalculic. However, there are other reasons for not being able to answer correctly, such as not knowing the number names.

Scatter some counters (between 5 and 10) and ask the pupil to estimate: *Guess how many there are?*

The child should be able to respond quickly without counting. Do not expect the exact amount but consider whether the answer is reasonable. A wildly inaccurate response indicates that they have little idea of magnitude.

Then ask the pupil to check the number of counters: *How many are there?*

Do they understand one-to-one correspondence? This means that they assign one number word to each counter. Note any strategies the child uses such as touching or moving objects as they are counted.

Repeat the activity with progressively larger quantities. When the child is investigating more than 20 counters, ask them to count them into a line and leave a small gap after each 10 counters. Ask: *How many are there? How do you know that?*

Watch to see that pupils are accurate in positioning the counters and that they count accurately. Make a note of any errors but do not correct them. Are they able to explain that a number is composed of some tens and ones, or do they need to count from the beginning to check?

COUNTING AND THE NUMBER SYSTEM

Check that the pupil can count forwards and backwards starting from 1, then from arbitrary starting points in the number sequence. It is particularly important to check that they can cross the decade boundaries; these are the points at which one group of ten ends and another begins.

Errors frequently occur at these crossover points. It may be that they miss out the decade number so that they count 28, 29, 31, 32 and so on. They may become stuck in a loop and return to the beginning of the decade each time they reach the boundary; for example they count 47, 48, 49, 41, 42, 43. Do not point out the error. Pupils who understand the number system do not make this error; teaching will need to start by establishing sound counting.

Then check the ability to count in tens, fives and twos. Always establish that they are able to count forwards before asking them to count backwards. If they cannot count forwards fluently and accurately, do not ask them to count backwards. Pupils need to be able to count forwards securely before being asked to work backwards, so teaching will start with establishing the forward counting sequence.

WRITING AND READING NUMBERS

Ask pupils to write some numbers before asking them to read them. The reason for checking writing before reading is that writing numbers involves recalling information rather than simply recognizing it. Errors in writing numbers are a useful indicator of knowledge of the number system and place value. First check that the pupil can write the numbers to 10 and then to 20, then work with larger numbers.

Reversing some, or all, of the digits 2, 3, 4, 5, 6, 7 and 9 is a common error. This may be due to immaturity, visual perceptual problems or specific learning difficulties.

Errors within the 'teen' numbers may indicate conceptual misunderstanding or auditory problems. Pupils may write a number in the order the words are spoken as in 61 for sixteen instead of 16. This indicates they do not understand that sixteen represents 1 ten and 6 units. Writing 60 instead of 16 indicates an auditory problem; they have not distinguished the difference between the 'ty' and the 'teen' ending.

It is important to include a variety of numbers, including those involving zero as a place holder. Pupils with numeracy difficulties often write multi-digit numbers as they hear them. For example 231 would be written as 200301. This indicates a lack of understanding of the place value structure. There is no need to investigate further as teaching would need to start with establishing understanding of the base-10 structure of the number system and the principle of exchange.

READING NUMBERS

Ensure that the child can read the numbers to 10, then to 20 before investigating larger numbers. Include numbers with zero as a place holder such as 608, or 530. If the pupil can confidently read three-digit numbers, check whether they are comfortable with thousands, tens of thousands and hundreds of thousands.

Basic calculation

Assessing calculation means checking both knowledge of the key facts and the ability to connect one fact to another by reasoning. The dot patterns on a conventional dice are useful as a vehicle for investigating knowledge of the concept of double and half as well as encouraging pupils to talk about numbers and their relationship to each other using comparative language.

EARLY CALCULATION

Early calculation is the ability to add or subtract one or two from a number. It also requires the use of the terms 'more than' and 'less than', which some pupils find confusing. Start by asking oral questions, then a few written questions.

A pupil who can count is usually able to add or subtract one from a number. They should be able to give the answer quickly without hesitation; however, some may have to start from the beginning and count all the numbers. What is 3 plus 1? The response will be: 'One, two, three, four.'

Pupils who are experiencing numeracy difficulties frequently find adding or subtracting two confusing because they are not sure whether to include the number they start on in the calculation. This problem usually occurs when the numbers are greater than ten. What is 2 more than 12? The pupil may answer: 'Thirteen'. The pupil has probably counted 'twelve, thirteen' under their breath. When asked to explain, they often reply that they are 'never sure whether to start with the 12 or the next number'.

KEY FACTS: DOUBLES AND NEAR DOUBLES

Knowing and understanding the doubles and near doubles facts, sometimes called the core patterns, is an important foundation that can be generalized to make calculations with larger numbers easier. This knowledge is also important for later work locating numbers on number lines. A double is a number that is obtained by adding a number to itself. A near double is a number that is one more, or one less, than a double number.

Give pupils oral and written questions to check their knowledge of the doubles to 5 + 5, then investigate their knowledge of the near doubles bonds. Even if they do not know the facts automatically, can they derive them from their knowledge of the doubles?

Investigating these numbers and concepts provides an opportunity to probe simple numerical thinking. If you know that 2 + 2 makes 4, how does that help work out what 2 + 3 makes? If the child can reason that 3 is one more than 2 so the answer must be one more than 4 which is 5, this indicates that they have basic reasoning skills.

The patterns on a conventional dice provide a useful model of the doubles and near doubles numbers to 6. Asking pupils to draw the patterns from memory can be enlightening. Pupils with poor spatial abilities will draw the dots a long way apart. Those with poor pattern recognition skills are likely to draw lines of dots, including for the numbers 4, 5 and 6.

Most pupils have seen a dice. If they have not, show it to them, allow them to talk about the numbers and then ask them to draw them.

KEY FACTS: NUMBER BONDS TO 10

The number bonds to 10 are the pairs of numbers that add together to make 10. It is essential that pupils know these facts as they are the basis of many of the calculation strategies with larger numbers.

Ask oral and written questions. Pupils should be able to quickly say which numbers make 10, and be able to recognize the bonds in various configurations and explain which bond is used. The bond 9 + 1 is used to answer the question 9 + ? = 10. The pupil uses the fact that 7 + 3 = 10 to complete 10 − ? = 7.

If the pupil knows the bonds of 10, find out if they can generalize this knowledge to larger numbers and explain how they are applying what they know. The key fact 4 + 6 = 10 can be used to work out 26 + ? = 30, or to find the answer to 40 + 60 = ?

Place value

The position of a digit in a number determines its value. In the base-10 system, the place value may be considered as a series of columns. The value of each column varies by a factor of 10 from the column adjacent to it. Pupils need to know the names hundreds, tens and units (HTU) which refer to the positions in a three-digit number. This basic structure of three columns designated HTU is repeated within the larger groups of thousands, millions, billions, etc. in the counting sequencing. Understanding place value is essential for grasping the quantities that numbers represent, and for accurate calculation.

CALCULATIONS INVOLVING TWO-DIGIT NUMBERS

Knowledge of place value can be assessed indirectly by checking pupils' ability to add and subtract numbers which require the use of tens and units. Adding a single digit to 10 should be accomplished easily. If the pupil cannot do this, teaching will need to focus on this aspect before proceeding.

There are two universal strategies which pupils need to master in order to calculate competently:

- bridging through 10

- partitioning.

Bridging through 10 is the strategy that uses the bonds of 10 facts to make calculations easier to handle. Numbers are separated into constituent parts and 10, or a multiple of 10, used as a 'bridge' to facilitate the calculation.

Partitioning is the process of separating numbers into components that make calculation easier. Assess pupils' ability to partition two-digit numbers into tens and units and three-digit numbers into hundreds, tens and units.

Multiplication and division

Pupils often learn the multiplication tables by rote without understanding the concepts that they represent, and do not realize that multiplication and division are inverse operations. As well as assessing knowledge of the multiplication facts, find out whether they can demonstrate what the facts represent. This is easy to check by asking them to use counters to show 2 threes. It is important to use this transparent language in which the number in each group (3) and the number of repetitions (2) is implicit. The forms 2 times 3 or 2 multiplied by 3 accurately describe the operation but do not make the concept of repeated groups absolutely clear.

The representation of 2 threes should be two groups with three counters in each group. If the pupil puts out 3 groups with two counters in each group, ask them what they have shown. Are they able to explain that there are 3 twos?

If pupils know their multiplication facts, explain that multiplication links to division. For example, 6 threes make 18, therefore 18 divided by 6 will be 3. Give oral and written questions to find out if they can apply this knowledge.

Formal written numeracy

Pupils may use standard written methods in a mechanical way without understanding the quantities the numbers represent. Sometimes they have difficulty remembering the steps in the procedures and the resultant errors can be illuminating for the assessor as they indicate how the pupil is thinking about the numbers.

First investigate addition and subtraction. Give the pupil written questions starting with two-digit numbers and then progressing to three-digit and four-digit numbers if the pupil is competent.

Examples of some common errors:

$26 = 8$ $\underline{45 + 9}$ $\quad 17$	The pupil has added the digits in the rows, and then added the results vertically.
26 $\underline{45}$ 611	The pupil has added correctly but does not understand place value. The result of $6 + 5$ was recorded as 11. Then the pupil worked out $2 + 4 = 6$ correctly but recorded 6 next to the 11.
$26 \quad = 8$ $\underline{45 + = 9}$ $\quad\quad 17$	The pupil does not understand place value so does not realise that the numbers are 73 and 18. Each digit is seen as unrelated to the others so they do not realise that 3 is part of 73. The pupil has worked out $8 - 3 = 5$ and then $7 - 1 = 6$. This error often occurs when pupils have been taught that you always take the smaller number away from the bigger number.

MULTIPLICATION AND DIVISION

First check multiplication methods. Many pupils learn the box method rather than the formal multiplication algorithm. Ask the pupil to multiply two small two-digit numbers such as 14 x 23. Ask them to set it out the way that they would use at school and to explain what they are doing as they do their workings.

It quite quickly becomes clear if the pupil understands what the numbers mean, or is simply carrying out a procedure.

Check division by giving the pupil simple examples that do not produce a remainder. These will involve a two-digit number divided by a single digit. Then check that they can divide by 10 and 100 using three-digit and four-digit numbers.

Finally investigate their knowledge of the concept of remainders by posing questions which will result in a remainder. Use examples in which a multi-digit number is divided by a single digit.

Planning

Write a short report of the findings from the assessment and summarize the information gained as succinctly as possible. It is helpful to use a list of the key areas of basic numeracy and mark the findings on that as both a quick reminder of what the weaknesses are and as a basis for planning teaching. See example of a Summary Numeracy Profile on pages 100–101.

Draw up a teaching plan consisting of clear goals and a realistic time frame. The **long-term goal** may either specify particular subject matter or be aligned with curriculum expectations.

The **medium-term plan** sets a goal for what is to be taught. Plan to teach one concept and its related topics over a fixed period of time. This will vary according to the extent of the difficulty. A rough guide is to allow ten lessons to teach three related topics. For example, if the concept is the bonds of 10, the topics might be modelling the bonds as triads, writing the equations represented by the triad formation and automatic recall of the bonds of 10. Set the medium-term goals out in a Teaching Plan Summary.

Summary of numeracy topics	Additional information
Set a realistic time in which to teach one concept. List three related topics to be covered. Example: Numbers to 10 • Counting to 10 • Dot patterns to 10 • Drawing dot patterns	Write brief notes on other factors that need to be considered, such as: • Behaviour and attitude • Oral skills • Literacy levels • Visual perception • Information from other professionals

Each lesson requires a detailed plan. The **individual lesson plan** focuses on one concept and the associated knowledge. The lesson plan sets out the aims of the lessons, essential vocabulary, equipment, and specifies the tasks, written work and games to be covered. Games play an important role in learning. Keep the structure of each lesson consistent so that pupils know what to expect. Write the pupil's name and age at the top the page and remember to record the date. Leave space on the right-hand side of the page to write brief notes during the lesson. These will include comments on the pupil's approach as well as any difficulties.

Structure of individual lesson plan

Objectives: set clear goals for the lesson

Equipment: list all the equipment required

Vocabulary: list key terms to be learned

Review: quick oral or written review of previous topic

New topic: teach new skill or concept: provide opportunity for pupil to use equipment, draw diagrams and write numbers

Word problems: present numerical information in context

Practice: mental and written examples

Game: reinforce new topic or revise previous work

Homework: short written task or game

Notes for next lesson: what needs to be revised; what to teach next

Be clear about what you need to teach and how you are going to teach it. Teaching takes place on several levels. Apart from the content of the lesson, which is concerned with mastery of the subject, each lesson should aim to improve underlying cognitive skills such as visual perception, use of language, memory and organization.

Plan the content of each lesson to match the level that the pupil is at, rather the requirements of the curriculum. Include teaching materials and activities designed to improve underlying cognitive skills such as visual perception, spatial orientation and memory. Provide opportunities for pupils to talk about their thinking and communicate their ideas in a variety of written ways including drawings, diagrams, charts and graphs as well as symbols.

Share the goals with the pupil. Being clear about what is expected of them, and how they will know they have reached their goal helps them to learn. It is dispiriting for anyone, especially a pupil who has difficulty, to be faced with a seemingly endless series of tasks without knowing how they are related to each other, or where they are leading.

Name	Date of birth
Date of assessment	Age at assessment

Number sense and counting

☐ Subitising

Estimating

☐ up to 10

☐ more than 10

Counting forwards

☐ in 1s

☐ in 10s

☐ in 5s

☐ in 2s

Counting backwards

☐ in 1s

☐ in 10s

☐ in 5s

☐ in 2s

Reading

☐ two-digit numbers (TU)

☐ larger numbers

Writing

☐ two-digit numbers (TU)

☐ larger numbers

Calculation

Addition +1, +2

☐ one more +1

☐ two more +2

Subtract -1, -2

☐ one less -1

☐ two less -2

☐ Dot patterns 1-6

Doubles

☐ up to 10

☐ up to 20

Near doubles

☐ up to 10

☐ up to 20

Bonds of ten

☐ addition

☐ subtraction

Number bonds 1-9

☐ addition

☐ subtraction

Bonds of tens

☐ addition (e.g. $47 + ? = 50$)

☐ subtraction (e.g. $70 - 6 = ?$)

Bonds of multiples of ten

☐ addition (e.g. $30 + ? = 100$)

☐ subtraction (e.g. $100 - 80 = ?$)

Name	Date of birth
Date of assessment	Age at assessment

Place value

☐ Principle of exchange

Ten plus a single digit/Tens plus

☐ 10 plus a single digit (10 + n)
☐ Tens plus a single digit (20 + n)

Bridging

☐ units + units (e.g. 8 + 5)
☐ tens + unites (e.g. 34 + 7)

Place value HTU

☐ value of each digit in a multi-digit number
☐ same units subtraction (e.g. 36 – 6)

Addition 10+

☐ 10 more

Subtraction –10

☐ minus 10

Subtraction strategies

☐ doubles
☐ bridging back
☐ counting on (shopkeeper's method)

Multiplication and Division

Multiplication

☐ demonstration of meaning

Key tables

☐ x5 ☐ x10
☐ Other tables
☐ x2 ☐ x4 ☐ x6 ☐ x8
☐ x3 ☐ x7 ☐ x9

Division

☐ grouping concept
☐ sharing concept

Word problems

☐ addition
☐ subtraction
☐ multiplication
☐ division

Formal Written Numeracy

☐ addition
☐ subtraction
☐ multiplication
☐ long multiplication
☐ short division

CHAPTER 8

What to Teach

Number sense has to be learned; it cannot be transmitted. This means that children need to engage different areas of the brain by exploring numbers using objects, drawing diagrams and talking about what they see and do. They need the help of more experienced people, whether adults or more competent children, to listen to what they have to say and discuss ideas.

Teaching involves guiding children to explore numbers in a systematic, multi-sensory way in order to establish secure foundations. Maths is a hierarchical subject and new concepts are built on existing concepts. Teaching starts at the point at which understanding has broken down. For pupils who are experiencing numeracy difficulties that is often right at the beginning which is counting. Adults and teenagers are often relieved to be allowed to return to what is often the root of the problem – misconceptions about the structure of the number system.

> Those who are not sufficiently fluent with earlier material should consolidate their understanding, including through additional practice, before moving on.
>
> (Department for Education 2014)

Counting and calculation

Counting is the foundation of numeracy. The base-10 system is a wonderfully efficient means of denoting every quantity from the miniscule to the gigantic, with every gradation in between. However, it takes time and exploration to master this system. It is imperative that pupils can count accurately and fluently. It is also imperative that they understand the patterns and relationships within the number system.

Experience has shown that numeracy difficulties often start with an inability to count in a meaningful way. Our understanding of what a number is, what is known as number sense, is so closely aligned to counting that it seems inconceivable that for some people counting means nothing more than a string of sounds.

It is often assumed that understanding of the number system will emerge from the process of counting. This is not necessarily the case. Too often counting is learnt by rote as a string of sounds. When written symbols are associated with the sounds, they have no meaning for the child beyond straight or squiggly lines. It is akin to learning music by only learning the names of the notes and seeing them written on a score, without ever hearing the individual sounds they represent nor realizing that they can be played as music and experiencing all the emotions that it evokes.

Children may memorize key facts such as the bonds of 10 but not understand that two sets are being combined. The result is that children do not grasp the relationship between the numbers. This has serious implications for calculation.

A **calculation** is the solution to a problem that involves processing numbers; it also refers to the process, or procedure that is used to compute the quantities. The arithmetical calculations are often referred to as the four operations, which are addition, subtraction, multiplication and division. At first children calculate by counting all the objects involved. Gradually they grasp the cardinal aspect of numbers so they can manipulate whole numbers. However, some pupils do not learn to do this and they continue to see a number as a 'clump' of ones. As a result every calculation is seen as an instruction to count.

Teachers may not realize that difficulties with calculation and more complex aspects of numeracy have their roots in failure to acquire basic counting skills, something a majority of children have mastered by the age of 5.

If pupils do not understand what a number is, they fail to perceive the patterns within and connections between numbers. They might know that $7 + 3 = 10$ but see $10 = 3 + 7$ and $10 - 3 = 7$ and $10 - 7 = 3$ as totally unrelated. The inability to make connections at this level means that they will not be able to perceive the structure within larger numbers, nor use their knowledge to derive new knowledge. Each calculation they are faced with is seen as a totally new problem.

It takes time for pupils to investigate ideas, and time for the cognitive changes to take place at a neural level in the brain. Information and ideas are more likely to be remembered if they are encoded in various areas of the brain, hence the need to include manipulation of objects, discussion, drawing and writing in order to involve as many areas of the brain as possible. In this way strong visual images are created which can be applied and generalized to more complex numerical scenarios.

Teaching programmes

Successful teaching programmes are systematic, structured and multisensory with an emphasis on developing flexible thinking as well as learning knowledge and skills. Concrete materials help children to see, explore and understand the number patterns and relationships as well as developing an idea of the size of numbers. Pupils use concrete materials to develop strong visual images of numbers, to stimulate thinking and to help develop the vocabulary and fluency in expressing their ideas. Contextual problems, often termed word problems, should be an integral part of any programme. Equipment is an effective way of providing a context, provided that it is used to provoke discussion, not merely as a calculating aid. It is also important to learn to use a variety of written and diagrammatic ways to communicate. Allow pupils enough time to think and construct their own explanations as this is a crucial part of concept of formation and the process of perceiving number as an abstract entity.

Work with the numbers to 10 to establish the meaning of number, both cardinal and ordinal, and the concepts of addition and subtraction before moving on to working with larger numbers which involve place value. Experience has shown that pupils who are able to discuss the internal structure of, and relationships between, small numbers, develop the logical reasoning skills and secure concepts that can be generalized to larger numbers. Communicating ideas in pictorial and diagrammatic form, as well as using symbols, is an essential part of creating understanding.

Plan the content of each lesson to match the level that the pupil is at, rather than the requirements of the curriculum. Include teaching materials and activities designed to improve underlying cognitive skills such as visual perception, spatial orientation and memory. Provide opportunities for pupils to talk about their thinking and communicate their ideas in a variety of written ways including drawings, diagrams, charts and graphs as well as symbols.

Pupils learn to think about numbers and what they represent, rather than seeing them as elements in procedural processes. Pupils develop strong visual images of numbers which help in developing reasoning skills and fluency in expressing ideas and recording them in different ways. The contexts can be ever more demanding. In this way pupils come to trust their own thinking as well as developing confidence in their ability to do the calculations so that they can generalize these skills as they work with increasingly large numbers and more complex ideas.

The most important consideration is that a programme is cumulative and coherent. Children need to learn within a structure that clearly links one concept to the next as the lessons progress. It is very easy to become overwhelmed by the detail provided in national curriculums and teaching programmes. Below is a simplified outline of the fundamental knowledge, skills and some of the vocabulary that children need to learn. It is designed to be comprehensible rather than comprehensive; to provide a starting point that is easy to follow.

Table 8.1 Overview of basic numeracy topics and key concepts

Numbers to 10	
Counting to 10	**Key concepts**
Count objects accurately	One-to-one correspondence – one number name is assigned to each item counted
Say number names	
Develop distinct visual images for each number from 1 to 10	The stable-order principle – number words have to be used in a fixed order when counting
Use equipment to model quantities	The cardinal principle – the final number in the count represents the total quantity in the collection
Draw diagrams of quantities	
Read numbers	The order-irrelevance principle – the order in which the objects are counted does not affect the cardinal value
Write numbers	The ordinal principle – the last number in a count represents the position in a sequence
Sequence numbers	
	There are patterns and relationships within numbers and between numbers

cont.

Numbers to 10

Calculation to 10	Key concepts
Basic calculation +1, −1, +2, −2	Numbers are composed of smaller numbers
Key facts:	Quantities can be changed by combining or separating them
• Doubles and near doubles bonds	Addition is commutative – the order in which numbers are added does not change the result
• Bonds of 10	The inverse relationship between addition and subtraction
• Bonds of all the numbers to 10	The same fact can be represented in different ways
Model key facts using equipment	
Record key facts as triads and in equations	

Numbers to 20

Counting to 20	Key concepts
Say number names and count objects accurately	The principle of exchange
Use base-10 equipment to exchange 10 ones for 1 ten	The difference between a number track (counting numbers) and a number line (measuring numbers)
Model the 'teen' numbers using equipment	Zero as a point on a number line
Record numbers as diagram	Locate numbers as points on a number line
Read numbers	

Write numbers

Sequence numbers to 20

Count forwards and backwards

Estimate quantities of up to 20 objects and check the estimate

Introduce the number line

Zero as the point at the beginning of the number line

Calculation to 20	Key concepts
Basic calculation $+1$, -1 $+2$, -2	Application of known facts to derive new facts
Universal strategies:	Concept of addition as combing two amounts or increasing a single quantity
• $10 +$ a single digit	
• Bridge through 10	Concept of subtraction as separating one quantity, or comparing two quantities in order to find the difference between them, or make one quantity equal to another quantity
Introduce concepts of addition and subtraction by using numbers in context	
Model calculations using equipment	
Record calculations as diagrams, on number lines and as equations	

cont.

Numbers to 100

Counting to 100	Key concepts
Number names and the structure of two-digit numbers up to 100	Base-10 structure of the number system
Counting forwards and backwards to 100	Rounding numbers
Counting in 10s	Finding rules governing sequences
Model numbers using equipment	Linking linear representation of number (the number track) to the area model of a number (number square)
Read and write numbers to 100	
Sequence numbers	
Locate numbers on a number line	
Round numbers to the nearest 10	
Introduce the empty number line and the partial number line	
Investigate number sequences generated by counting in 2s, 5s or 10s	
Introduce the 100 square	

Numbers to 100

Calculation to 100	Key concepts
Universal calculation strategies:	New facts can be derived from known facts using the knowledge of the structure of the base-10 system
• Generalizing from key facts (e.g. $2 + 3 = 5$ therefore $20 + 30 = 50$)	Numbers can be partitioned (separated) into components to make calculations easier
• Extend bridging through 10 to any two-digit number	Numbers can be rounded to the nearest 10 to allow quick calculation of an approximate result
• Partition numbers into tens and units	
• Calculate an approximate answer against which to check the result of a calculation	

Multiplication and division

Multiplication	Key concepts
10 times a number	Multiplication as repeated addition (repeated groups)
Understand that 5 times a number is half of 10 times a number	The array model of multiplication
Universal strategy for multiplication: Quickly derive any multiplication fact by reasoning from 10 times and 5 times a number	The area model of multiplication
	Link the array model to the area model of multiplication

cont.

Multiplication and Division	
Division	**Key concepts**
Relate division to the array model of multiplication	Inverse relationship between multiplication and division
Demonstrate division as splitting a quantity of objects into groups so that each group will have a specified number of objects	Division as grouping
Demonstrate division as sharing a quantity of objects equally between a specified number of groups	Division as sharing
Division with remainders – use numbers in context to make the effect of remainders clear	The concept of remainders – they may need to be taken into account in a calculation, or discarded, according to the context
	The area model of division links directly to the long division algorithm
Place value	**Key concepts**
Model two- and three-digit numbers using base-10 equipment	The concept of place value – the position of a digit in a multi-digit number determines its value
Read and write three-digit numbers	The concept of zero as a place holder
Zero as a place holder	Extend the principle of exchange to multi-digit numbers
Introduce the place value grid	
Addition involving the need to exchange quantities	

Subtraction involving the need to decompose quantities on the place value grid

Decomposition involving multi-digit numbers

Model and record the changes between place values

Represent place value as a structured grid with groups of hundreds, tens and units (HTU) repeated within the larger categories of thousands and millions

Extend the place value grid to include thousands and millions

Standard written methods

Addition and subtraction

Key concepts

Relate the formal methods to concrete models

Apply place value knowledge to standard algorithms

Work out approximate answers before completing formal calculations in order to check results

Apply the principle of exchange and decomposition

Multiplication

Key concepts

Model multiplication as the box method using equipment

The box method shows how division relates directly to the array and area model of multiplication

Record the box method as a diagram and show calculations

Relate the standard multiplication algorithm to the box method

contr.

Division	Key concepts
Model division as the box method using equipment	Division is the inverse operation to multiplication
Record division using the box method as a diagram	The box method relates directly to the array and area model of multiplication
Long division – relate the standard algorithm to the box method	
Use equipment to model and carry out the standard long division procedure	
Remainders – model and record problems involving division with remainders	

---------------------------------- CHAPTER 9 ----------------------------------

How to Teach

Teaching and learning numeracy requires patience. Numeracy is not difficult if you are allowed to explore objects, compare them, quantify them, talk about them, combine them and separate them, draw diagrams and jottings and learn to communicate your ideas in symbols. It becomes difficult to learn if you are chivvied to move on to the next concept before you have grasped the initial concept; if your achievements are constantly compared to others and you are reminded that you are not learning as quickly as they are; if you are shouted at when you make mistakes and berated because you are confused. When this happens anxiety sets in and you are unable to learn; in time you come to hate numbers.

Learning numeracy requires experiment and engagement with ideas. These can easily be achieved by providing pupils with equipment and asking them to do things and talk about what they are doing and record their ideas. This is called multi-sensory teaching. Teaching numeracy requires introducing new questions and ideas and guiding pupils to develop numerical concepts and knowledge through using equipment and developing vocabulary. Teachers do need to teach the conventional symbols, signs and calculation procedures. However, this is best done by exploring the concepts first and then using mathematical notation to express the ideas. In this way the symbols are meaningful rather than simply a collection of squiggles on paper and memorized rules about how they fit together.

If pupils can develop a sense of curiosity about how the world is organized – first within the classroom setting and later transferring that knowledge to the wider world around them, they will be well on the way to becoming numerate.

The 21st century requires people to be able to solve problems. Traditional arithmetic teaching placed the emphasis on getting the correct answers. Problem solving requires the ability to ask the right questions, and then to reason logically to find the answer. From the very earliest years, teaching needs to establish the habit of thinking about numbers and their meanings and expressing those thoughts in a variety of ways.

Earlier chapters covered how to plan lessons and what content needs to be learned to acquire basic numeracy. This chapter describes how to use multi-sensory techniques.

It is not possible to provide details of everything that needs to be taught and learned. However, some of the key concepts are used as examples. There are a variety of teaching programmes available that provide comprehensive instructions on what and how to teach. The examples given below are part of the teaching programme at Emerson House in London and available in the book *The Dyscalculia Solution: Teaching Number Sense* (Emerson and Babtie 2014).

Structured, cumulative, multi-sensory teaching

Numeracy needs to be taught in a way that is structured, cumulative and multi-sensory.

Structured means that topics are taught in a logical order. It also means that each lesson follows a coherent structure: review previous knowledge, introduce a new topic, and provide opportunities to investigate the topic and communicate ideas using concrete, diagrammatic and written methods.

Cumulative means that each new concept or idea builds on previous knowledge. It is essential that pupils master a concept before embarking on a new one that depends on the prior knowledge. For example, it is essential to be able to count accurately before being able to calculate. Cumulative also means that work starts with real objects; the concrete model is then represented in pictorial or diagrammatic form and finally recorded as a written procedure.

Multi-sensory means using as many senses as possible in order to activate different brain areas and establish reliable memories. This was discussed in Chapter 2. Make teaching multi-sensory by encouraging pupils to use real objects which they can manipulate to develop meaningful images. It is essential that pupils talk about what they are doing as they model numbers and calculations. In this way they improve their cognitive skills such as visual perception, logical reasoning, memory, and organization as well as developing mathematical vocabulary and knowledge. Recording thinking in the form of sketches, diagrams, charts, graphs, on number lines and as equations is a vital part of the multi-sensory process.

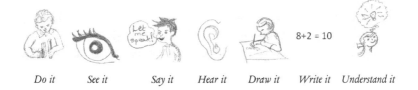

Do it   See it   Say it   Hear it   Draw it   Write it   Understand it

Summary guidelines for teaching

- Be clear about **what** you need to teach and **how** you are going to teach it.

- Keep **concise records** of what happens in each lesson and what needs to be reviewed.

- Set **clear goals** with the pupil and explain the **criteria for success** in achieving them.

- Keep the structure of **each lesson consistent** so that pupils know what to expect.

- Follow a progression from **concrete** to **diagrammatic** to **written** within each lesson.

- Provide **real objects** including counters, Cuisenaire rods and base-10 equipment so that pupils can build strong **visual images** of concepts and calculations.

- Encourage pupils to **talk** about what they are doing and record their thinking.

- Allow pupils **time** to explain ideas **in their own words** so they can gradually build up definitions that make sense to them.

- Guide pupils to communicate their ideas in a variety of ways using **drawings, diagrams, charts, number lines and equations**.

- **Games** play an important role in learning as they provide the opportunity for purposeful practice and encourage a positive attitude to maths if they are approached in a way that the pupil finds enjoyable.

- Plan activities to help **improve underlying skills** such as visual perception, categorization, analysis, memory and organization.

- The teacher keeps questions and **instructions short and clear**.

- Use **full sentences** and relate answers back to the original question.

- The teacher uses **correct vocabulary** from the start to model numerical vocabulary.

- Introduce **word problems** right from the beginning, both ready prepared and encourage pupils to make up their own word problems.

- Work with **small numbers** until the concepts of basic counting and calculation are firmly established.

- Gradually encourage **pupils to take responsibility** for their own learning by deciding how they will tackle problems and which methods to use to communicate their thinking.

Suggested equipment

Base-10 equipment

Base-10 equipment (Dienes blocks) consists of cuboids (based on the 1cm³ unit cube) used to make clear the relative size of the numbers 1, 10, 100 and 1,000. They should all be the same colour.

Bead strings

Large beads are arranged in alternating groups of two colours to show repeated groups of 10 beads. The beads are used to reinforce one-to-one correspondence in counting as well as to make calculation strategies clear.

They are particularly useful for demonstrating cross-over points at the decade boundaries.

Counters

Use small objects for counting and representing numbers. They should be all the same colour and size, and easy to pick up. Any objects of a regular shape and size can be used. Glass nuggets make attractive counters, which often interest even the most reluctant child.

Cuisenaire rods

Cuisenaire rods are coloured cuboids of proportional length. The colours help to identify rods of different length. The rods are versatile pieces of equipment. They are used to represent both the whole numbers from 1 to 10 in basic number work, and fractions and ratios when parts of numbers are introduced.

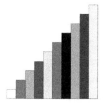

Dice

Conventional dice are used to represent quantities and as the basis for developing an understanding of numbers relationships. Numbered dice are used in activities and games to practise reading digits and to generate numbers, including multi-digit numbers.

Ruler

Use rulers that show the whole numbers aligned with the vertical mark that demarcates each interval.

Some rulers have the numbers printed in the space between the lines. This representation can cause confusion between the concept of the number track and the number line.

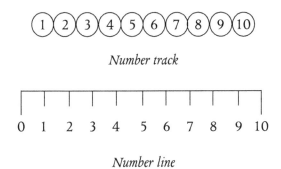

Number track

Number line

Word problems

Word problems help to develop logical reasoning, which is the basis of problem solving and an essential life skill. Logical reasoning depends on the proposition that if certain information is true, then a particular result must follow. In a world that is increasingly driven by data, it is also important to be able to analyse information and select what is relevant.

Numbers should be used in context wherever possible so that pupils experience numbers used in a meaningful way to solve problems. Equipment puts numbers into context if it is used to explore and discuss numbers and their relationships. (Equipment should not merely be used as a calculating aid.) Try to create word problems that are of interest to the pupils and ensure that they make up their own problems. Real world topics can range from toys and animals to sport, meals and timetables. 'The fantasy world of fairy tales and even the formal world of mathematics can provide suitable contexts for a problem, as long as they are real in the student's mind' (Van den Heuvel-Panhuizen 2001).

Problem solving involves identifying what the question is, selecting the relevant information, planning effective action and reviewing the result to make sure it makes sense. The key to successful problem solving is asking pertinent questions to guide thinking.

- What do I want to find out?

- What information do I have?

- How can I summarize the relevant information?

- How do I express the problem in numerical terms?

- Can I show the information more clearly in a diagram, chart or graph?

- What is a sensible estimation of the result?

- Which arithmetical operation is required? Is there more than one possibility?

- Does the answer make sense?

Word problems need to form part of every lesson rather than being seen as a separate category, often unrelated to the concepts being taught. Sometimes pupils are taught to classify word problems into certain types, and to identify the appropriate method of calculation from trigger words. It is better if they develop a strategy that allows them to tackle problems in a systematic, understanding-based way in order to discover the meaning as well as work out the result.

It is a good idea to work with small numbers and increase the complexity of the information contained in the problem. This places the focus on working out what is required. Too often pupils guess which operation to use from the size of the numbers, reasoning that they are unlikely to be asked to multiply large numbers therefore the question probably involves addition or subtraction.

Pupils often find that making up their own word problems requiring use of a particular operation is surprisingly difficult. Encourage them to use concrete materials to model the question with the equipment representing the things that they are thinking about.

An example of increasing complexity in a simple word problem:

> Adam had 3 apples. He got 2 more. How many apples did he have?

In the second example below, increased detail and the inclusion of extraneous material means that the child has to work to extract what is relevant. This also tests knowledge of categorization by referring to fruit rather than apples.

> Adam bought 3 red apples and 4 packets of biscuits at the supermarket. Then he went to the corner store and bought a bottle of milk and 2 green apples. How much fruit did he buy?

In the third example below, there is far more information to analyse and the calculations become more complex. This kind of problem is known as a two-step problem. Representing the information in tabular form will make it much easier to understand.

> Adam bought 3 red apples and 4 packets of biscuits at the supermarket. Then he went to the corner store and bought a bottle of milk and 2 green apples. Apples cost 10 pence each, milk is 50 pence a bottle and a packet of biscuits costs 20 pence. How much did Adam spend?

Multi-sensory teaching

The activities described below are samples of how to teach some of the key concepts. Remember, it is not a case of doing an activity and moving on to the next concept. The work must be consolidated by frequent practice, especially with missing number equations to build flexibility, and by solving problems. Pupils also need to use jottings to help their thinking and record it in diagrammatic and symbolic forms.

Numbers to 10

Establish a sound understanding of the numbers to 10 before asking pupils to deal with larger numbers.

COUNTING TO 10

Teach pupils to count accurately by placing objects in a line. They say each number word as they place the object. Then the teacher asks, '*How many are there?*' Often the pupil will need to return to the beginning of the line and count all the objects again. It is important not to rush this work as it takes time to understand that the final number word in the count represents both the total quantity of objects (cardinal value) and the position in the counting sequencing (ordinal aspect).

Pupils also need to learn to compare numbers. Pupils may find the concept of comparison difficult. Up to this point they will have used comparative terms such as more, less, larger, bigger and smaller to refer to the relative physical size of objects. Now they learn that quantities can be compared using the same terms. It is through plenty of practice counting out objects, comparing the quantities and talking about what they see that they gradually come to understand what it means to say that one number is smaller or larger than another.

In the activity called 'Number tracks', pupils learn to compare numbers in a structured way by seeing two lines of counters. These are counted onto a structured track composed of ten circles. This subliminally introduces the idea of the base-10 structure of the number system long before it is explicitly taught.

Goal: To count to 10 accurately

Learning objectives:

- Recognize numerals 1 to 3.
- Count to 10.
- Synchronize number names with objects counted.
- Order objects as they are counted.
- Compare quantities.
- Use comparative language.

ACTIVITY: NUMBER TRACKS

Equipment

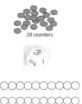

20 counters (all the same colour)

Dice marked 1 to 3

Board with one empty track for each player

Players take turns to roll a dice and take the quantity of counters indicated. They place the counters on their track. The winner is the first person to reach the end of the track.

Encourage the players to talk about what they are doing and seeing during the course of the game. They should use their own words. The teacher introduces new words if the pupils do not know them.

The example shows play and suggests the kind of questions and comments to encourage.

How many counters are there?

Who has more counters?

Can you compare the lines of counters?

How many more counters do you need to have the same as the other player?

Can you check how many counters you have?

Example showing play
Round 1: Player A throws 3, Player B throws 3

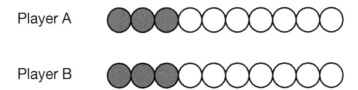

Player A

Player B

Player B says: *I have the same number of counters as player A. We both have the same number of counters. I have 3 counters and player A has 3 counters.*

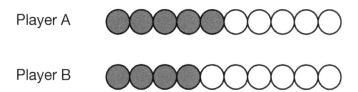

Round 2: Player A throws 2, Player B throws 1

Player A

Player B

Player A says: *I have more counters than player B. I have 1 more counter than Player B. I have 5 counters and player B has 4 counters.*

Player B says: *I have less counters than player A. I need 1 more counter to have the same number as Player A.*

DOT PATTERNS

Pupils need to be able to visualize the quantities that numbers represent. They need to develop the concept of relative size and to think in terms of components. Dot patterns provide visually distinct images that enable them to do this easily.

Goals: To develop visually distinct images of each number from 1 to 10

To understand the relationships between numbers in the sequence from 1 to 10

Learning objectives:

- Recognize, recall and draw the dice patterns 1 to 6.

- Construct dot patterns for numbers 7, 8, 9, 10.

- Use comparative and positional language.

- Use the terms double and half in relation to patterns and numbers.

- Describe the relationship between a doubles number and its components.

- Use the term 'a double number' to mean a number that results from adding a number to itself.

- Use the term 'a near-double number' to mean a number that is one more or one less than a double number.

- Draw accurate dot patterns of doubles and near doubles patterns.

- Match numerals to dot patterns.

Mathematics is often described as the study of pattern. All patterns contain ideas of regularity. This may be achieved by repetition of shape, or take the form of change in a structured way according to a rule. Much of understanding numeracy is concerned with grasping the patterns and relationships within and between numbers and the number structure.

Dot patterns are visually distinct representations of numbers. The dot patterns emphasize the cardinal value of each number whilst making it clear that numbers are composed of smaller numbers. Grouping the numbers into clearly defined patterns helps to overcome the tendency for pupils who struggle with numeracy to see numbers as strings, or clumps of ones; the dot patterns provide both external and internal structure to the numbers.

The dot patterns represent the doubles and near doubles number to 10; these are sometimes referred to as the core patterns. Two important concepts are inherent in the core patterns – the commutative property of addition and the inverse relationship between addition and subtraction.

The dot patterns are derived from conventional dice patterns by reasoning to produce doubles and near doubles images for all the numbers from 1 to 10. It is essential that pupils are guided to develop the dot patterns for themselves by analysing the conventional dice patterns and then generalizing those findings. Pupils should be allowed to experiment with different representations so that they realize that a particular arrangement of objects is not a property of a number; the patterns are produced for clarity and to make it easier to visualize numbers and their components when they are used in calculations. (Colour is another attribute that is not a property of a number but it is used in Cuisenaire rods to make it easier to identify rods of differing lengths.)

ACTIVITY: DISCOVERING DOT PATTERNS

Equipment

55 counters (all the same colour)

Ask the pupil to use counters to make the patterns that appear on a dice. If the pupil has not seen a dice, or cannot remember them, then give them a dice to follow. Pupils with poor pattern recognition skills may have great difficulty doing this exercise. The orientation of the patterns does not affect the value; however, for clarity in distinguishing the numbers and their component parts it is best to present them in a way which emphasizes the distinctive structure of each image as shown below.

Ask the pupil to point to the pattern of 2 and the pattern of 4 and say: '*Tell me what you see*'. Often children are able to explain that 4 is made of a 2 and another 2, or 4 is made of 2 twos. If they cannot see this, spend some time helping the pupil to model the pattern of 2 and adding to it to make the pattern of 4 whilst talking about what they are doing. They need to synchronize words and actions so that if they say '4 is made of 2 and 2' they make the patterns and combine them in the pattern as they are speaking. Introduce the language of double and half. Remember that it is important to use full sentences to clearly establish the meaning as in 'Four is double two' and 'Two is half of four'.

Once they are comfortable talking about the relationships between 2 and 4 and can express it in different ways, ask them to discuss the relationship between the pattern of 3 and the pattern of 6.

Discuss the ways in which the larger number is made of two smaller numbers, or two smaller numbers are combined to make the larger one.

Then ask them to make some new patterns. Say: 'Can you make a pattern that is double 4? Use the pattern of 4.' Encourage them to talk about what they are doing. If they make a pattern that consists of two lines of 4 counters, point out that this is not wrong, it is a pattern of 4. However, it does not make it clear that the pattern is derived from the original pattern of 4. (The difference is important in developing a distinct visual image which makes the repeated pattern explicit and can be used in calculation later.)

Next ask the pupil to make the pattern that is double 5.

Ask the pupil to put the new patterns in order in the sequence.

Ask them to name the numbers they have made. Do they notice that 7 and 9 are missing? Some pupils recite the number sequence from 1 to 10 but do not realize that they have no pattern for 7 and 9. This is an indication that the pupil has little idea of the concept of number and will have to be very carefully taught before they can progress in maths. The teacher will need to guide them to discover the omission for themselves by drawing attention to each number pattern in turn.

Once the pupil is aware that 7 and 9 are missing, discuss the patterns that are one more than, or one less than, a double such as 3. They use their own words to explain that 3 is between 2 and 4, 3 is one more than 2, and 3 is one less than 4.

Now consider the pattern of 9. Say: 'Tell me where 9 is in the sequence.' When the pupil has responded that 9 is between 8 and 10, ask them to describe the relationship between 8 and 9, then the relationship between 9 and 10. They should use the language of before and after, and explain that 9 is one more than 8 and 1 less than 10. Explain that you want a pattern that is a near double. The easiest way to achieve this is to make the pattern of 10 and remove one counter to reveal that 9 is made of 4 and 5. Then work the other way, starting with the pattern of 8 and add one counter to make 4 and 5. Of course it does not matter whether the pattern is 4 and 5, or 5 and 4, as the value will remain the same.

Finally the pupil makes the pattern of 7, going through the same process of discussing its position in the sequence. It is easiest to guide them to the near doubles pattern of 4 and 3 if they start with the pattern of 8.

Pupils need plenty of practice to establish strong images which are useful memories. Work on associating the pattern with the numeral by doing matching activities so that the spoken word and written numbers trigger a meaningful image and association not just with the quantity, but also its component parts. In this way the patterns become useful tools for calculation.

Calculation: Key facts

There are a few key facts which pupils need to know 'off by heart'. Pupils who learn these facts by deriving them from experimenting with objects, and working with them to achieve automaticity, will develop visual images which reduce the load on memory. Understanding the relationships will also enable them to apply this knowledge to calculation strategies with larger numbers. Pupils need to have plenty of practice working with the key facts and using them in word problems.

The dot patterns provide a spatial representation of the number bonds, making the numerosity of the components clear. Pupils also need to understand the linear representation of numbers. Use Cuisenaire rods to provide a distinctive model which places more emphasis on the proportions of the components.

The triad, or number triple, formation helps pupils grasp the relationship between a number and its components and will be applied in strategies with multi-digit numbers. The triad is described below in the work on bonds of 10. Pupils also need to be familiar with all the different ways that each number bond can be represented in equations, as described below.

A triad showing the relationship between 7 and the components 4 and 3.

DOUBLES AND NEAR DOUBLES BONDS TO 10

Allow pupils plenty of time to learn the doubles and near doubles bonds by exploring concrete representations, doing calculations and solving, and composing, word problems.

These key facts are evident in the structure of the dot patterns. Pupils who have derived the core patterns and drawn diagrams will be able to use the images to help them work out calculations involving doubles and near doubles. Explore the doubles and near doubles bonds using triads and link them to equations in the manner described below for work on bonds of 10.

Goal: To use cuisenaire rods to model the doubles and near doubles bonds

Learning objectives:

- Model the doubles bonds to 5 + 5 using Cuisenaire rods.

- Draw diagrams of the model to show the doubles bonds to 5 + 5.

- Write equations for the doubles to 5 + 5 = 10.

- Use Cuisenaire rods to model the near doubles bonds by relating them to the doubles bond.

- Draw diagrams of the model to show the near doubles bonds to 4 + 5 = 9.

- Write equations for the doubles to 4 + 5 = 9.

Work systematically through the doubles bonds. The pupil needs to investigate each bond and describe it in different ways as they build up the model. There are two ways of representing the model. The pyramid model emphasizes the aspect of double and half of each number. The staircase model makes it clear that each doubles number is 2 more or less than the numbers adjacent to it.

ACTIVITY: DOUBLES BONDS AND NEAR DOUBLES BONDS

Equipment

Cuisenaire rods

Pencil

Squared paper

First explore the doubles bond. Start with 1 + 1 = 2. The teacher puts out a single cube (white) and says: '*This is 1. Can you show me double 1?*' Encourage the pupil to talk about what they are doing and seeing in their own words. They need to communicate ideas such as one and one makes two; two is double one.

They model all the doubles bonds to 5 + 5, discussing each one.

The pupil draws a diagram of the doubles patterns on 1cm² squared paper and colours it in to match the colours on the Cuisenaire rods. Encourage pupils to draw the diagram without using a ruler to draw attention to, and hence associate, the length of the rod with the number of squares. Some pupils find this very difficult and may need to draw around the rods to help them. Finally pupils write the equation that each bond represents.

$$1 + 1 = 2$$
$$2 + 2 = 4$$
$$3 + 3 = 6$$
$$4 + 4 = 8$$
$$5 + 5 = 10$$

Now explore the near doubles bonds. Pupils reason logically to describe the relationship between the doubles and near doubles bonds. They work with one fact at a time. Do not ask them to incorporate all the bonds in one large model as it is visually confusing.

The teacher demonstrates what is required by using rods to show 1 + 1 = 2, then placing the rods for 1 + 2 = 3 immediately below it and saying: 'Tell me what you see.'

The pupil uses their own words to convey the idea that 1 and 1 makes 2. One more than 2 is 3, so 1 and 2 must be one more than 2. Therefore 1 plus 2 equals 3.

The pupil then constructs each near doubles bond by relating it to the preceding doubles bond. They draw diagrams and write the equations.

Pupils need to consolidate their knowledge by doing calculations, modelling them, and solving word problems. Remember that meaningful and purposeful practice leads to automaticity.

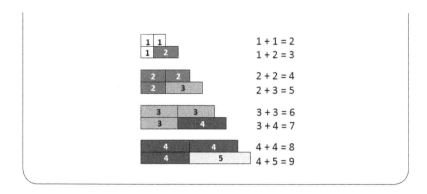

BONDS OF 10

It is essential that pupils know and understand the bonds of 10. This knowledge is fundamental to the calculation strategy of bridging through 10 and through multiples of 10 as well as hundreds and thousands. Without this knowledge pupils are left with little alternative but to see each calculation as an instruction to count – however large the quantities involved.

Goal: To learn the bonds of 10

Learning objectives:

- Represent the linear relationship between the bonds of 10 using Cuisenaire rods.

- Use triads to show the relationship between a numbers and its components.

- Demonstrate that the bonds of 10 encapsulate addition and subtraction facts.

- Write the equations represented by the bonds of 10.

- Recognize bonds of 10.

- Recall bonds of 10 quickly.

ACTIVITY: LINEAR MODEL OF BONDS OF 10 USING CUISENAIRE RODS

Equipment

Cuisenaire rods

Pencil

Squared paper

Colouring pencils

Use Cuisenaire rods to explore all the different ways you can make 10 by combining two rods. Pupils model the number sequence from 1 to 10 as a 'staircase'. They then build a second sequence.

Slot the two sequences together to form a shape so that the orange rods (ten) are at the outside of the shape. The resulting shape shows all the bonds of 10 and makes the commutative property of addition visible.

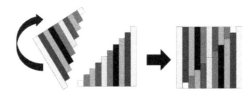

Allow the pupil to explore the shape and rotate it to show both vertical and horizontal bonds of 10. Give pupils plenty of opportunity to construct and deconstruct bonds of 10 and talk about what they are doing and seeing. It is important that they see the pattern that as one number increases, the other decreases, and that the bonds 1 + 9, 2 + 8, 3 + 7 and 4 + 6 are repeated, though in a different order to give 6 + 4, 7 + 3, 8 + 2 and 9 + 1.

Pupils use squared paper to draw a diagram of the bonds of 10 starting with 1 + 9. They write the equation that each bond represents next to it.

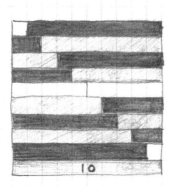

$1 + 9 = 10$
$2 + 8 = 10$
$3 + 7 = 10$
$4 + 6 = 10$
$5 + 5 = 10$
$6 + 4 = 10$
$7 + 3 = 10$
$8 + 2 = 10$
$9 + 1 = 10$

ACTIVITY: BONDS OF 10 AS TRIADS AND EQUATIONS
Equipment

10 counters (all the same colour)

Triad mat

Pencil and paper

A triad, also called a number triple, is a way of representing number bonds in a written form which emphasizes the relationship between the numbers. Initially teach a triad as a diagram with an oval at the top, and two lines branching out from the same point on the oval to meet two lower ovals. Once pupils understand the concept they need not draw the ovals and they will only use the lines. This form will be used later with calculations with multi-digit numbers.

Pupils make the dot pattern for 10 and then split it into two components. They use counters on a triad mat, then draw a diagram to record what they have done by writing the number 10 at the top of the triad and drawing the constituent dot patterns in the lower ovals. Then they write the bond in numbers using the triad formation as shown below. Finally they write the equations that the triad represents. It is important that they move the counters as they describe what each equation means.

The teacher demonstrates what is required. It is important to explain your thinking as you move the counters, draw the diagrams and write the numbers. Start with the bond 10 = 5 + 5. Many pupils are confused by this form as they have been taught procedures such as 'the answer always goes on the right'. They need to learn that there are many different ways of representing the same idea. The equal sign indicates that information on each side has the same value. It is a concept that pupils need to understand before they can deal with more complex calculations.

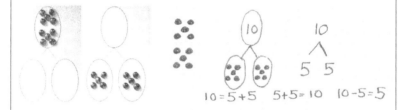

$$10 = 5 + 5 \qquad 5 + 5 = 10 \qquad 10 - 5 = 5$$

Ask the pupil to model all the bonds of 10 in a similar way. It is best that they start with 10 = 5 + 5. They use their own words to talk through the process as they make the patterns, draw them, write the triad and write the equations.

Then they investigate each of the possible bonds of 10 using the same procedure. It does not matter which pair of numbers the pupil chooses to make. Some quite quickly see the pattern that as one bond increases, the other decreases. Other pupils do not see any links between one fact and another. They need to be given the time to explore, to move the counters, record the results and talk about what it means. The process cannot be hurried. It is only by grappling with the problem and making sense of it for themselves that pupils will be able to store the information in as meaningful memories that they can draw on for future use.

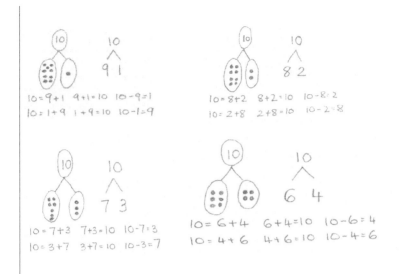

10=9+1 9+1=10 10-9=1
10=1+9 1+9=10 10-1=9

10=8+2 8+2=10 10-8=2
10=2+8 2+8=10 10-2=8

10=7+3 7+3=10 10-7=3
10=3+7 3+7=10 10-3=7

10=6+4 6+4=10 10-6=4
10=4+6 4+6=10 10-4=6

Pupils need plenty of practice with the bonds of 10, in written exercises, solving word problems and playing games which require applying knowledge of the key facts.

BONDS OF ALL THE NUMBERS TO 10

It is helpful, but not essential, for pupils to know the bonds of all the numbers to 10.

Once pupils know the key facts of doubles and near doubles, and the bonds of 10, there are very few other facts to learn. Pupils who can reason about numbers can quickly derive the additional facts from the known facts. Provided that they understand the commutative nature of addition, there are only 12 further facts to learn. Six of these involve adding 1. These are 1 + 3, 1 + 4, 1 + 5, 1 + 6, 1 + 7, 1 + 8. There are four facts that involve adding 2. These are 2 + 4, 2 + 5, 2 + 6, 2 + 7, and 2 + 8. The final facts are 3 + 5 and 3 + 6.

*Diagram showing all the number bonds to 10 highlighting the
doubles and near doubles bonds and the bonds of 10*

Number lines

A number line represents numbers as point on a line. Whole numbers
are marked at regular intervals. Fractions of numbers can also be
shown. They lie between the whole numbers. Number lines such
as rulers and tape measures are used to measure length or distance.
The numbers on a number line are often referred to as the measuring
numbers.

The distinction between the measuring numbers and the counting
numbers is an important one. It can be easily taught in the activity
described below (Hop and Jump). Counting numbers are used to
find the quantity of discrete objects such as people or counters, or
things that are imagined. Measuring numbers are used to quantify
continuous amounts such as length, distance, time or temperature.

Too often the number line is introduced before children have
grasped the meaning of the counting numbers. It is best to delay
introducing the number line until pupils can confidently count to 20
with understanding.

The number line requires the use of the concept of zero as the
point of origin. Often young children are taught that zero means
'nothing', which leads to later confusion when they meet zero as
a place holder in the place value structure. It is difficult to explain
the concept to a young child, or even an adult who is confused.
However, it can be demonstrated.

Understanding number lines is essential for all measurement and
for representing information on graphs. The number line is also a
versatile calculation tool which is particularly useful for work with
large numbers. It is a very powerful tool to use to support thinking
and reasoning about numbers. Encourage pupils with numeracy

difficulties to make jottings using number lines to help keep track of calculations. It takes time to learn to use number lines but it is well worth doing.

A number track consists of discrete numbers. Each number occupies a definite space on the track. The number track starts at 1.

A number line represents continuous numbers. Whole numbers are marked at regular points on the line. Fractions can be marked between the whole numbers. The number line starts at 0 (zero).

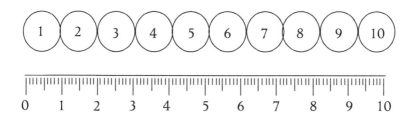

The number track and the number line

USING NUMBER LINES

Goal: to use number lines to support numerical thinking

Learning objectives:

- Clarify the difference between the number track and the number line.

- Draw arcs to indicate distance on a number line.

- Construct a number line.

- Locate points on an empty number line.

- Understand the partial number line as a section of the number line.

- Use number lines to describe calculations.

ACTIVITY: HOP AND JUMP

Equipment

Each player has a number track numbered to 20
(best to use circular spaces)

Ruler

Paper and Pencil

Dice (1 to 6)

One counter
for each player

Give each player a track numbered to 20. It is best to show the spaces as circles as this makes the distinction between the spaces clear. Each player uses a ruler to draw their own number line marking the numbers to 20. Do not tell the players that the line will start with 0 (zero). Many people, adults as well as children, make the mistake of writing 1 at the beginning of the line. They need to discover the error for themselves and think about what it means. The process of discussing it will help them to establish the meaning far better than telling them the answer.

Players take turns to throw the dice, move along the track by either hopping or jumping, then recording the move as an arc on the number line. The winner is the first person to reach or pass 20.

A hop is a movement of one; a jump is more than one. Players may either move in a series of hops, which means that they are counting in ones, or they may jump the distance shown on the dice, which is the equivalent of calculation. If they hop in ones they record each hop on the number line, then draw a single, larger arc to show the distance moved on that turn.

It is important that players do not slide the counter along the number track; each move needs to be a distinct arc in the air from the starting number to the next position.

Often players want to place an extra circle at the beginning of the number track and mark it zero (0). Allow them to do this then ask them how many circles they have. The answer will be 21, which means that they have added 1. Ask them to stand up and do two forward hops calling out as they count each hop. They will say the words 'one' and 'two' as they land. No one ever says zero as they start the movement. Then ask them to delete the extra circle so that there are only 20 circles.

When pupils can confidently do this activity on a marked number line, play the same game using a number line on which the intervals of the whole number are marked but only the numerals 0, 5, 10, 15 and 20 are shown.

A game in play

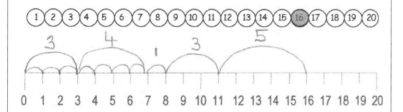

Player A

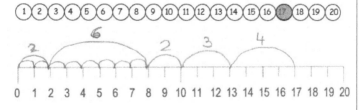

Player B

ACTIVITY: LOCATE A NUMBER ON AN EMPTY NUMBER LINE

Equipment

Pencil and paper

An empty number line is a number line on which there are no points marked. Pupils should draw lines without using a ruler. Locate 14 on the number line. Start by marking the 0 (zero) at the beginning of the line and 20 at the end of the line.

Now find the mid-point on the line and mark it correctly. Pupils use their own words to reason to find 14. *Half of 20 is 10 so the half way point is 10.*

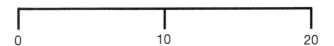

Find the mid-point between 10 and 20 which is 15. *I know that 5 is half of 10 so the mid-point between 10 and 20 will be 15 because 10 and 5 is 15.*

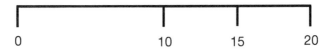

14 is less than 15 so it will lie between 10 and 15. It is only 1 less than 15 so it will be quite close to 15.

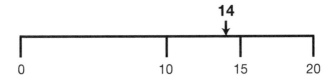

ACTIVITY: BRIDGING THROUGH 10 ON THE NUMBER LINE

Equipment

Cuisenare rods

Pencil and paper

The bridging through 10 strategy is used to add numbers where the result will cross a decade boundary. This strategy can be adapted for use with larger numbers.

The pupil models the calculation using Cuisenaire rods and talks about and records what they are doing.

The teacher says: '*24 and 8 equals what? Record the calculation on an empty number line. Mark 0 and 24 on the number line. Make an arc to show 8 and write a question mark to show where the answer will be.*' Using the word 'what' and the question mark directs the pupil to the point at which the answer will be found. It is important that the pupil says that the answer will be more than 24 to help locate the position of the answer.

Model the calculation using Cuisenaire rods

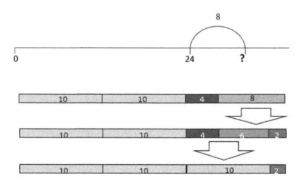

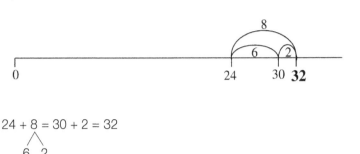

Record the steps in the calculation on a number line and as an equation

$24 + 8 = 30 + 2 = 32$

Place value

The number system is a place value system. The most widely used place value system is the base-10 system. All numbers, however large or small, are made up from the individual digits 0, 1, 2, 3, 4, 5, 6, 7, 8 and 9. The value of each digit in any number with more than one digit depends on its position, or place, in that number. The place value structure can be shown as a diagram with a series of columns. The value of each column varies by a factor of 10; the value of each column is 10 times larger than the column to the right and 10 times smaller than the column to the left. The names of each column give the value of the number. There are three columns named HTU (hundreds, tens and units). The names HTU are repeated within each of the larger categories of thousands, millions and more.

MILLIONS			THOUSANDS					
Hundreds	Tens	Units	Hundreds	Tens	Units	Hundreds	Tens	Units
H	T	U	H	T	U	H	T	U

Place value columns showing the repeated pattern of HTU

The names are spoken as hundred millions, ten millions, millions, hundreds of thousands, tens of thousands, thousands, hundreds, tens, units. It is customary to demarcate repeated groups of three numbers

(HTU) in order to make them easier to read. The convention in the UK and the US was to use commas whereas people in continental Europe used a full stop. In order to avoid confusion, the international standard is to leave a space. However, this is impractical in the classroom when children's handwriting and number spacing is erratic. It is advisable to continue to use a comma. The full stop is now used universally to denote a decimal fraction of a number. Later pupils learn the use of the standard form which obviates the need for demarcations.

Be wary of using directional language such as numbers getting bigger as they *move to the left*, or smaller as they *move to the right*. The numbers do not move; their value increases. Teachers should also be aware that the place value grid and the number line are different representations of number. The number line sequences numbers from 0 to infinity (in theory) counting from left to right.

Place value grid

Millions			Thousands					
H	T	U	H	T	U	H	T	U

Numbers getting larger ⟵———————————

Number line

```
 ┌┬┬┬┬┬┬┬┬┬┬┬┬┬┬┬┬┬┬┬┬┬┬┬┬┬┬┬┬┬┬┬┐
 0      10      20      30      40      50      60
```

———————————⟶ Numbers getting larger

BASE-10 AND THE PRINCIPLE OF EXCHANGE

Understanding the place value system depends on understanding the principle of exchange.

The principle of exchange means that a specific number of items can be exchanged for a single item that has the same value. This principle is used in many everyday situations. For example, in American currency 10 one cent coins can be exchanged for 1 dime which is a single coin worth 10 cents. It is easy to demonstrate the principle of exchange by using base-10 equipment. This is sometimes called Dienes equipment after the inventor Zotlan Dienes.

Base-10 relationships underpin the meaning of multi-digit numbers in the decimal system. Dienes equipment provides a model that makes it easy to visualize what the quantities are. Dienes equipment is based on metric measurements. The relative size of each piece equates to its relative place value. The unit cube, worth one, measures 1cm^3. The 10 stick is a cuboid that is 10 cm long; the 100 square is 10cm^2. The large cube of 10cm^3 is worth 1,000. It is usually referred to as the thousand block.

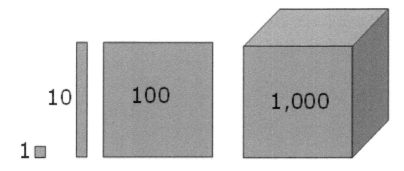

Allow children time to explore the relationships between the pieces of base-10 equipment in an unstructured way, as well as directing them to notice the relationships. Simply using the equipment as construction blocks to build whatever they want to helps to start them thinking about the relative size. Teach the relationships formally encouraging pupils to find out how many ones (units) are the same as one long stick, or how many ones you need to cover the square.

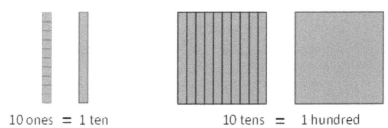

10 ones = 1 ten   10 tens = 1 hundred

Investigate the thousand block by modelling it as hundreds, then tens and finally units. This order represents the order of the place value positions.

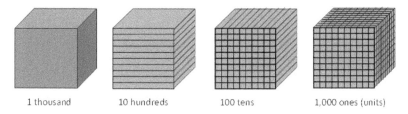

| 1 thousand | 10 hundreds | 100 tens | 1,000 ones (units) |

Goal: To understand the place value structure

Learning objectives:

- Investigate the value of each digit in a multi-digit number.

- Use base-10 equipment to demonstrate numbers in linear and spatial formats.

- Build and describe two-digit numbers using base-10 equipment.

- Use base-10 equipment to show that the value of a digit depends on its position in the number.

- Understand the use of 0 (zero) as a place value holder.

- Build numbers on the place value grid.

- Exchange on the place value grid.

- Record numbers in diagrams and equations.

ACTIVITY: INVESTIGATE PLACE VALUE USING BASE-10 EQUIPMENT

Equipment

Base 10 equipment (hundreds, tens and units)

Digit cards (0 to 9)

Paper and pencil

0 – 9
Digit cards

Build two-digit numbers

Start by investigating two-digit numbers. Do not use numbers containing a 0 (zero) at this stage. First make the linear model of the number. Then show how the equipment can be used to give a spatial representation. Align the tens sticks vertically and put the unit cubes in the number pattern. Ask pupils to build a variety of numbers, to draw diagrams and to write the numbers, making it clear that they are composed of tens and units.

Build 34

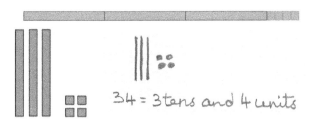

34 = 3 tens and 4 units

This is also an opportunity to introduce the use of tally marks. Demonstrate that it is easier to see how many ten sticks there are if they are put in the tally formation. Five is represented by 4 vertical lines and a diagonal line to show 5 ⵜⵜ. This is often called a gate check as the image looks like a traditional barred gate. Continue to use number patterns for the units.

Build 65

65 = 6 tens and 5 units

Build three-digit numbers

Ask pupils to build a variety of three-digit numbers. Provide three-digit cards and ask them to arrange them to make different numbers. They model each number, draw it and write the equation to show what each digit in the number represents.

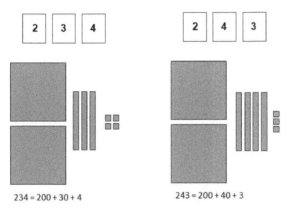

234 = 200 + 30 + 4

243 = 200 + 40 + 3

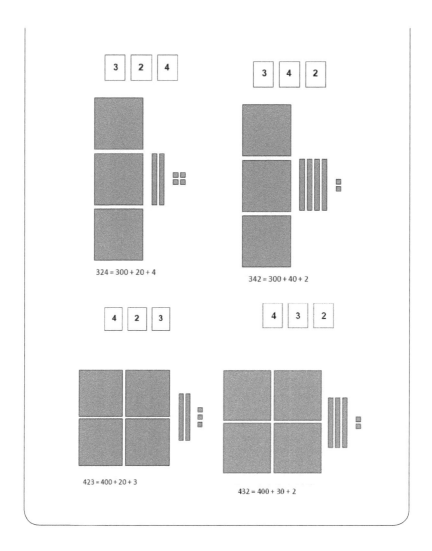

324 = 300 + 20 + 4

342 = 300 + 40 + 2

423 = 400 + 20 + 3

432 = 400 + 30 + 2

Numbers on the place value grid

The place value grid is a diagram with three columns headed H T U for hundreds, tens and units. Model three-digit numbers on a place value grid drawn on plain A4 paper. Encourage pupils to draw their own place value grids but provide them with one if they have difficulty drawing. Pupils build and record a variety of three-digit numbers.

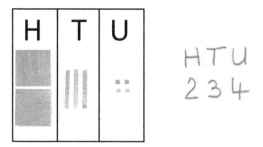

0 (ZERO) AS A PLACE VALUE HOLDER

Teach the concept of zero as a place holder. Zero occupies a position in a number to ensure that the other digits in the number are in their correct places. Never use the word 'nothing' to describe zero as children with poor number sense then think it can be ignored. Terms such as *no* tens, or an *empty* place indicate the *absence* of something which has to be taken into account.

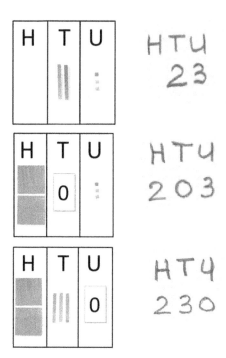

Investigating the effect of zero as a place holder

Pupils investigate the importance of zero in a number by making numbers on the place value grid. They compare numbers which have zero in different positions and record the numbers under place value headings, and as equations. Use a digit card with 0 to emphasize that zero is a place holder.

Exchange on the place value grid

Start with two-digit numbers, and then move on to working with three-digit numbers. First practice the exchanges required when a quantity is added to the existing number. Then explore the changes involved when a quantity is subtracted from a number. This is usually referred to as decomposition, but it is not necessary for pupils to use the term if they find it too difficult. The can use their own words to describe the changes. Pupils who are able to demonstrate the addition or subtraction of numbers using base-10 equipment, and record what they see, will find that it exactly represents the procedures involved in the standard addition and subtraction algorithms.

Demonstrate exchange on the place value grid:

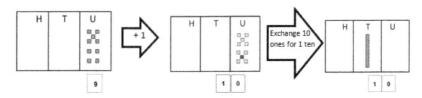

APPLYING KNOWLEDGE TO DERIVE NEW FACTS

Pupils who know the bonds of the numbers to 10 and understand the structure of the number system can apply their knowledge to calculations with larger numbers.

Generalizing from key facts
    Doubles and near doubles
      $3 + 3 = 6$ $300 + 300 = 600$
      $30 + 30 = 60$ $23 + 3 = 26$
                            $2,300 + 300 = 2,600$

Bonds of 10

$10 - 2 = 8$ $10 - 4 = 6$

$100 - 20 = 80$ $90 - 4 = 86$

$1,000 - 200 = 800$ $9,000 - 40 = 8,960$

Bridging

Bridging through 10

$5\,6 + 7 = 50 + 10 + 3 = 60 + 3 = 63$

\4/   3

Bridging through 100

$470 + 50 = 400 + 100 + 20 = 500 + 20 = 520$

\30/   20

Applying triads to larger numbers

Partitioning

$$57 + 32 = 50 + 7 + 30 + 2$$
$$= 80 + 9$$
$$= 89$$

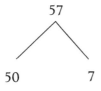
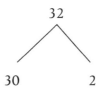

CHAPTER 10

How Parents Can Help

Play with your child

Play with your child. This is the best way to help them to learn. Play involves all the elements of successful learning – a purposeful attention to an activity, talking and listening to discuss ideas with other people and a feeling of pleasure in the task. Play helps children develop a growth mindset, the positive attitude that challenges are to be embraced and that mistakes are an opportunity to learn.

Convey a positive attitude to maths and learning. Many adults have developed a dislike of maths or a fear of it; however, do not pass this on to your child. Make sure that you are not one of the adults who makes comments like *I can't do maths, I was never any good at maths, maths is boring* or *maths is difficult.* Maths is actually fascinating and great fun if approached in the right way.

Set an example of being calm and organized. Teaching your child how to keep their toys tidy involves learning to plan where to put them and how to sort them, which are the first steps in learning to solve problems. Later teach them how to plan ahead by managing their time. These essential life skills also provide an opportunity to learn about time and set goals as well as making sure you have time to do what you want to do as well as what you have to do.

This chapter gives some suggestions for activities and games, as well as ways to help children learn to manage their time and organize themselves and their activities. It is intended to remind parents of some of the activities that have got lost in the digital age as well as suggesting new ones. The list is by no means comprehensive.

From the moment a child is born parents look at them, smile at them, cuddle them, bounce them and talk to them about what is going on around them. Parents are not taught to do this. It is a natural instinct. Unfortunately there are circumstances where this does not happen and this has detrimental effects on the child's language development.

Language and vocabulary develop from hearing words modelled by adults in meaningful situations. Children learn to name things by looking at objects and trying to name them. It has been estimated that it takes about 800 repetitions of a word before an infant knows it. At first the infant babbles unintelligibly. The proud parent encourages them to make more sounds by responding. For example the infant points at a dog and makes gurgling sounds and the parent says the word *dog*. Every time the child sees a dog and gurgles, the parent says the word *dog*, often accompanied by a comment such as 'Well done, you said dog.' They see dogs, pat dogs, talk about dogs, look at pictures of dogs in books and gradually the infant learns that the word *dog* applies to an animal with four legs and a tail. Of course this also applies to other animals, so the child needs to learn to distinguish a dog from other quadrupeds. Being able to identify similarities and differences is an important skill which gradually develops from discussions between a child and a more experienced person, whether child or adult.

The number words are also introduced in conversations about the child's world. The child hears the number words related to things such as the number of legs on people, animals or chairs, to abstract things such as birthdays or bedtime, as well as seeing them written on the bus or the door of the house. Talking about numbers as part of everyday life is the best way of starting to make children aware of the way numbers are used in the real world.

A child learns an enormous amount before they start school. Apart from naming things, they learn words to describe the relative position of objects. These include up, down, over, under, next to, top, bottom, right and left. They learn words to describe attributes such as size and speed: the same as, different, little, lot of, small, big, slow, fast, and use the comparative terms smaller, bigger, larger, slower, faster. Children need to understand this vocabulary in order to make sense of instructions.

Rhythm is also a pre-learning skill. Developing rhythm requires attention to sound patterns and distinguishing them and then repeating them using motor skills such as movement of hands, or singing.

Children need to be able to sequence things, which means putting them in the correct order. Before they learn the sequences involved in literacy and numeracy, they learn to organize things in a structured way by putting toys or shapes in order of size, or colour or shape.

Early years
Numbers

Use numbers in conversations in practical everyday situations whenever you can. Identify and use different kinds of numbers, such as the number of wheels on a car, a number on a house or numbers used in counting out biscuits to share.

Sorting and matching

- Do simple jigsaw puzzles.

- Buy, or make, simple shapes (triangle, square or circle) in three different sizes and colours. Ask your child to find all the smallest shapes, or all the red shapes, or all the circles. Ask them to sort them according to a particular attribute.

- Play card games with matching pairs of pictures.

- Ask your child to help sort the washing and to match pairs of socks.

- Give your child some saucers and ask them to put a cup on each one.

Paying attention

- Play I Spy with attributes of objects rather than letter sounds.

- Play Animal, Vegetable or Mineral. Player A thinks of an object and says whether it is an animal, vegetable or mineral. The questioner has to ask questions to find out what player A is thinking of by gradually working through different properties.

- Do spot-the-difference activities.

- Encourage children to draw.

- Give children pictures to colour in.

Sequencing

- Build structures with coloured blocks.

- Thread different colour beads in repeating patterns.

- Do dot-to-dot activities.

- Play simple track games with a conventional dice with dot patterns.

- Help children learn the days of the week and the months of the year.

Rhythm

- Traditional nursery rhymes provide a pleasurable way of teaching number names and sequences, such as 'One, two, buckle my shoe' and 'Ten green bottles'.

- Clapping simple rhythms.

- Hopping.

- Skipping.

Childhood

Numbers

Once a child starts school make sure that they use numbers in practical everyday situations. Time offers a rich source of number discussion, from the time shown on the clock to the way time is parcelled into days, months and years. Food shopping provides an opportunity to consider weights and measures on packages and get a sense of how much a kilo feels like, as well as learning how to use money. Sport provides the context for talking about and comparing numbers in many ways, such as the number of people on a team and scores.

Planning and following instructions

Cooking requires planning and carefully following instructions as well as introducing the weighing and measuring. Use construction toys such as Lego and Meccano. Play card games including rummy, patience, Uno, Top Trumps. Play dice games.

Play board games that involve thinking about directions and strategies as well as those involving travelling around a number track. A few suggestions are Monopoly, Mastermind, draughts (checkers), Othello, chess, mancala, Continuo.

Jigsaw puzzles can be used to teach the systematic search required for problem solving. Teach children to talk about the pieces they have and to sort them into those with straight sides and those with no straight sides. Then they construct the outside edge of the puzzle by looking at each piece and talking about the colours they see and working out what colour they need to look for. Initially they may want to use the picture on the box to help; then show them how to approach the puzzle without looking at the picture.

Movement and direction

Sport is an excellent way to develop the spatial and directional language required for numeracy, as well as developing movement and perceptual skills. Too often in schools the children who are best at sport get the most practice because they are selected for teams. As they get more practice they inevitably become better. If your child is not one of the school sports stars, help them find an activity they enjoy and can become proficient at outside school.

Music

Learning a musical instrument, or taking part in a choir, develops memory, movement and organizational skills. Children need to practise regularly; taking charge of their own practice times helps them develop personal responsibility.

Poetry

Too often children's exposure to poetry in the home stops with nursery rhymes. Encourage them to read poems and learn to recite them.

Organization and time-keeping

Help your child construct a simple timetable for after school activities. Call it the 'More time to play plan'. Children often feel weighed down with all the things they *have to do*. This is especially true for those who are experiencing any kind of learning difficulty and feel they are always trying to catch up but never getting there. The idea is to show the child that they have time to play and get everything else done if they plan it. Of course they then need to do their tasks at the appointed time and stop when the time is up.

Write a list of what is needed for each school day. Older children can do this themselves. Teach them to prepare everything on the list the evening before. This simple rule prevents the morning getting off to a bad start because there is a rush to leave the house. It also means that they have the equipment they need at school.

Homework

Homework should be a chance to review something that has been learnt before, or to apply new skills to fresh problems in order to consolidate understanding. Too often it causes misery for the child and becomes a battleground between parent and child.

Approach homework calmly by instituting the following regime. The child needs to take responsibility for completing the homework. Establish a set amount of time to do homework. Twenty minutes a night is sufficient for a child of 7 or 8. The child decides what time they are going to start work and collects everything required before then. The child sets a timer for the allotted time. They stop work when the timer goes off.

Sticking to this routine helps them develop a sense of how long it takes to do a task, and what a length of time feels like, without having to break their concentration and check the clock. The slight change in emphasis from having to finish a piece of work in a particular time, to seeing how much you are able to achieve in a fixed time, reduces stress. Children who stick to this routine are likely to find it much easier to cope with exams as they know how much they are able to do and are not afraid of the time pressure.

If they find it difficult the teacher needs to know what they find difficult, so it is not helpful if the parent provides the answers. Parents can help by encouraging the child to talk about what they are doing and suggest ways of tackling the problem if the child is completely stuck. In numeracy the best way to do this is to provide suitable equipment that can be used to model the problem.

Teenagers

Time management and organization are essential skills for teenagers to master. They need to extend their competence from managing their own time and possessions on a daily basis to dealing with planning study schedules and developing strategies for learning. These are called study skills.

The basis of study skills is the same as for any problem solving: identify what the question is, select the relevant information, plan effective action and review the result to make sure it makes sense. In this case the question is what you need to learn. The school may have provided a syllabus, if not the pupil needs to find out, either from the teacher or from information published on the curriculum or exam syllabus, in the case of national exams.

The pupil selects what to learn or revise. The next task is to draw up a study schedule covering several months, as well as a detailed weekly timetable to establish what to study when.

Teenagers need to take responsibility for their own learning. The text below is written to be shared with your teenager. Parents can encourage but the teenager needs to have a sense of control.

Effective studying is hard work but it can be extremely satisfying. It requires determination and persistence. However, the good news is that once good study skills are established they will be with you for life. Determination and persistence enable you to overcome adversity. They are attributes that are rarely taught and they are not examined by our education system but they are prized by employers. They are attributes that will equip you well for life.

Don't leave revision to the last minute and then try and study all day. It does not work.

Exam revision starts on the first day of your course. You must get organized. Aim to order your life, not compulsively or excessively, but to enable you to function at your best and *enjoy it.*

Time management is the basis of all study skills. Set realistic goals to be achieved in or by a stated time. The term SMART target has become ubiquitous. (It stands for small, measurable, achievable, realistic and timed.)

This means breaking the task into manageable topics and working out a way to check when you have learnt the information. It is important to allow a realistic amount of time to learn and revise the material. The sense of achievement you get from completing what you set out to do will help to motivate you to do more.

Understanding is the key to successful learning. If you understand what you are doing as you go along, recalling the information will not be a problem. You must ask for help if you do not understand. If one person cannot help you, then ask someone else. In mathematics it is often helpful to use equipment to explore what a question means and to help you develop visual images of the concepts rather than seeing mathematics as a series of symbols and procedures.

Learn to take efficient notes so that you come to the end of the year with topics and vocabulary summarized in a succinct format which uses images as well as words. These might be on index cards, or a few sheets of A4 paper. There are various systems for devising short notes – some students like the spatial arrangement of mind maps or spidergrams on cue cards, others prefer the linear arrangement of the Cornell method in which both linear notes and diagrams are combined.

Whatever the system you prefer, the idea is the same – reduce lessons, books and written notes to the key concepts. It is not the notes themselves which help you remember (though they are useful revision tools for refreshing your memory) but the effort involved in constructing them. The more actively you work on information the easier it is to remember.

RESOURCES

The internet provides information on a vast range of organizations involved in education. There is so much that it is bewildering. The lists below include both large national and international organizations as well as some of the smaller institutions and professional bodies.

Many of the major organizations have links from their websites to the organizations that they recommend so these are not repeated in the list below. There is also information about some of the bodies offering information about support for learning difficulties other than numeracy.

Programmes for dyscalculia and numeracy difficulties

Beat Dyscalculia
Beat Dyscalculia is a highly structured, multi-sensory numeracy intervention programme for primary school children. It can be used with older pupils.

www.beatdyscalculia.com

Catch Up™ Numeracy
This is a structured one-to-one intervention for pupils who struggle with numeracy.

www.catch-up.org

Dynamo Maths
Dynamo Maths is an interactive online resource designed for primary-aged children who have dyscalculia or numeracy difficulties.

www.dynamomaths.co.uk

Emerson House

The Dyscalculia Solution: Teaching Number Sense (Babtie and Emerson 2014)

This is a practical written guide to a multi-sensory approach to teaching pupils with dyscalculia or numeracy difficulties.

Numicon

A primary maths programme to develop numeracy. It uses a multi-sensory approach to develop understanding and reasoning skills.

https://global.oup.com/education/content/primary/series/numicon/?region=international

Unicorn

This is a structured programme for the development of numeracy and the remediation of maths difficulties and dyscalculia.

www.unicornmaths.com

UK resources

Children and Families Act 2014

www.legislation.gov.uk/ukpga/2014/6/pdfs/ukpga_2014
0006_en.pdf

Department for Education (2014)

National Curriculum in England: Mathematics Programmes of Study.
www.gov.uk/government/publications/national-curriculum-
in-england-mathematics-programmes-of-study/national-
curriculum-in-england-mathematics-programmes-of-study

Department of Education Northern Ireland

The official website of the Department of Education Northern Ireland.
In collaboration with other organisations it created the Northern Ireland Curriculum website (see below).

www.deni.gov.uk

Dyslexia-SpLD Trust

The Dyslexia-SpLD Trust is a collaboration of voluntary and community organizations with funding from the Department for Education to provide reliable information to parents, teachers, schools and the wider sector. It acts as the important communication channel between government, leading dyslexia organizations, parents, schools, colleges, teachers and the sector.

www.thedyslexia-spldtrust.org.uk

Education Scotland

Education Scotland is the national body in Scotland for supporting quality and improvement in learning and teaching. It was established in 2011. (See also Enquire)

www.educationscotland.gov.uk

National Numeracy

National Numeracy is an independent UK charity working to develop effective approaches to improving numeracy, especially amongst those with low levels of numeracy.

There are links to other relevant organizations from the National Numeracy website.

www.nationalnumeracy.org.uk

National Centre for Excellence in the Teaching of Mathematics (NCETM)

NCTEM collaborates with a wide range of agencies, institutions and associations devoted to maths education. One of their aims is to raise the status and professionalism of educators involved in teaching maths. There are links to their partner and stakeholder organizations from their website.

www.ncetm.org.uk

Ofsted (Office for Standards in Education, Children's Services and Skills)

Information about how the curriculum changes affect the way that Ofsted inspects assessment in schools.

Ofsted Inspections: Clarification for Schools (2014)

www.gov.uk/government/publications/ofsted-inspections-clarification-for-schools

Inspecting Schools: Handbook for Inspectors (2014)

www.ofsted.gov.uk/resources/school-inspection-handbook

STEM
STEM stands for science, technology, engineering and maths. There is a wide variety of government agencies, businesses, universities and charitable organizations engaged in encouraging more pupils to study the STEM subjects. Two organizations that provide a starting point to find out about what is available are the National STEM Centre and the STEM Education Centre London (SECL). The National STEM Centre provides teaching and learning resources and is situated at York University. The SECL evolved from the Science Learning Centre at the Institute of Education in London. It offers professional development, research and consultancy to the STEM education community.

www.nationalstemcentre.org.uk

www.stemedlondon.org.uk

US resources

ACT
ACT is the admissions and placement test that is one of the measures that colleges and universities use to select students. It also produces assessments for children in elementary schools and high schools. The organization that administers the tests is ACT Incorporated which provides a wide range of information and research on education and careers.

www.act.org

American Psychiatric Association
DSM-5 (Diagnostic and Statistical Manual of Mental Disorders) is the latest manual of mental disorders for mental health

professionals in the US. It is used internationally as a standard for mental health disorders.

www.dsm5.org

Center on the Developing Child – Harvard University
The Center on the Developing Child aims to find scientifically valid ways to help improve education for children facing adversity. They have produced the free booklet *Enhancing and Practicing Executive Function Skills with Children from Infancy to Adolescence* (2004). This guide contains ideas for games and activities to help children and teenagers develop executive function and self-regulation skills. These skills are critical for learning.

www.developingchild.harvard.edu/resources/tools_and_guides/enhancing_and_practicing_executive_function_skills_with_children

College Board
The College Board is an organization that manages standardized assessment tests for colleges and universities as well as developing and administering assessments for schools. It aims to help students prepare for higher education by providing resources and advice on all areas of college admissions. Amongst the programmes it runs are the SAT and the Advanced Placement Programs.

www.collegeboard.org

Common Core State Standards (2010) *The Common Core State Standards for Mathematics*
Washington, DC: Governors Association Center for Best Practices (NGA Center), Council of Chief State School Officers (CCSSO)

www.corestandards.org/math

Department of Education
The official website of the US Department of Education. It includes information about policy, the law, student loans and grants. There are links to many educational initiatives including NAEP (see below).

www.ed.gov

National Center for Education Statistics (NCES)
The NCES collects and analyses educational data in the US and other nations. It is part of the US Department of Education and the Institute of Education Sciences. The NCES is responsible for conducting the National Assessment of Educational Progress (NAEP) assessments.

http://nces.ed.gov

National Assessment of Educational Progress (NAEP)
The NAEP measures comparative national standards in education. The progress of students across the US is assessed by testing representative samples of students in Grades 4, 8 and 12 every year. Every four years there is an assessment of pupils aged 9, 13 and 17 in mathematics and reading to monitor long-term trends.

http://nces.ed.gov/nationsreportcard

Individuals with Disabilities Education Act (IDEA 2004)
The Individuals with Disabilities Education Act (IDEA) is the law that governs services to children and young people with disabilities in the US. The US Department of Education website provides a 'one-stop shop' for information and resources related to IDEA and other associated regulation.

http://idea.ed.gov

NCLD (National Center for Learning Disabilities)
The NCLD provides comprehensive information and resources as well as working to promote public awareness of learning disabilities and strengthen legal safeguards.

One of the programs offered by NCLD is called Understood. This is an online resource for parents of children with learning difficulties and disabilities. It gives clear advice and explanations of legal and educational issues.

www.ncld.org

www.understood.org

World Health Organization ICD-10

International Statistical Classification of Diseases and Related Health Problems – 10th revision. This is the most recent edition of the medical reference directory that is used as a diagnostic tool internationally.

www.who.int/classifications/icd/en

Yale Center for Dyslexia & Creativity

The Yale Center for Dyslexia and Creativity at Yale University is a research institute as well as a leading source of advocacy and information to better the lives of people with dyslexia. It is part of the Yale School of Medicine.

www.dyslexia.yale.edu

Numeracy: online resources and useful organizations

About Dyscalculia

This public information website provides scientific information about dyscalculia for parents, teachers and policy-makers.

www.aboutdyscalculia.org

Association of Teachers of Mathematics (ATM)
The Association of Teachers of Mathematics was established in 1950 to encourage the development of mathematics education. ATM was founded by Caleb Gattegno who did much to popularize the use of Cuisenaire rods.

www.atm.org.uk

Brian Butterworth
Updates on the latest research into dyscalculia, and links to resources.

www.mathematicalbrain.com

The British Dyslexia Association (BDA)
The BDA campaigns for a dyslexia friendly society. The BDA also provides information about dyscalculia and numeracy difficulties.

www.bdadyslexia.org.uk

National Helpline: 03334 054567

Cambridge University
Free enrichment material (problems, articles and games) at all Key Stages for mathematics.

www.nrich.maths.org

Centre for Educational Neuroscience (CEN)
The Centre for Educational Neuroscience brings together three previously distinct disciplines – developmental psychology, neuroscience and education. It is a joint venture by University College London, Birkbeck College London and the Institute of Education.

www.educationalneuroscience.org.uk

Dyscalculia Centre
Provides information and resources about dyscalculia.

www.dyscalculia.me.uk

Dyscalculia.org
Math Learning Disability Resource
An educational organization 'dedicated to advancing understanding and treatment of specific learning disabilities in mathematics, also known as dyscalculia'.

www.dyscalculia.org

Dystalk
Discussion forum for issues related to dyslexia, dyspraxia and dyscalculia. Interviews with professionals in the field and lists of resources.

www.dystalk.com

Enquire

Enquire is the national advice and information service for additional support for learning in Scotland. It is managed by Children in Scotland and funded by the Scottish Government.

www.enquire.org.uk

Helpline: 0345 123 2303

Hamilton Trust

Hamilton Trust is an Oxford-based education charity that provides resources and training for primary teachers.

www.hamilton-trust.org.uk

Learning Skills Foundation

The Learning Skills Foundation identifies, supports and promotes effective learning skills of all kinds. **'How to learn'** is just as important as **'What to learn'**.

www.learningskillsfoundation.com

Northern Ireland Curriculum

An information website managed by the Northern Ireland Council for Curriculum Examinations and Assessment (CCEA). It provides easily accessible information including downloadable guides on *Assessment for Learning - A Practical Guide* and *Parents' Guides To Assessment.*

www.nicurriculum.org.uk

Number Catcher

Free online game involving basic arithmetic concepts – calculation, sets and the logic of multi-digit numbers.

www.thenumbercatcher.com/nc/home.php

Numbersense

Free online interactive games to practise basic number sense, including pattern recognition and counting, bonds of 10, locating points on a number line and telling the time. Provided by the Institute of Education London.

www.number-sense.co.uk

Stanislas Dehaene, INSERM U562, Paris
Updates on the latest research and lists of further academic articles to read.

www.unicog.org

Other learning difficulties: UK organizations providing information and support

Attention Deficit Disorder Information and Support Service (ADDIS)
ADDIS provides information about attention deficit hyperactivity disorder to anyone who needs assistance – parents, sufferers, teachers or health professionals.

www.addiss.co.uk

British Association of Behavioural Optometrists
Behavioural optometrists use lenses and vision training to facilitate the development of a more efficient and complete visual process.

www.babo.co.uk

The British Dyslexia Association (BDA)
The BDA campaigns for a dyslexia friendly society. The BDA provides support and advice about dyslexia and related specific learning difficulties. The BDA has a network of local Dyslexia Societies and a network of volunteer befrienders.

www.bdadyslexia.org.uk

National Helpline: 03334 054567

Contact a Family
Contact a Family provides a range of fact sheets and has a network of volunteer reps to help families with disabled or special needs children.

www.cafamily.org.uk

CreSTeD

CReSTeD (The Council for the Registration of Schools Teaching Dyslexic Pupils) helps parents, and those who advise them, to choose schools for dyslexic children. All schools included in the Register are visited regularly.

www.crested.org.uk

Dyslexia Action

Dyslexia Action provides services and support for people with dyslexia and literacy difficulties. Dyslexia Action provides assessment, education and training.

www.dyslexiaaction.org.uk

The Dyspraxia Foundation

The Dyspraxia Foundation offers support and resources to dyspraxics and their families.

www.dyspraxiafoundation.org.uk

The Dyslexia-SpLD Trust

The Dyslexia-SpLD-Trust is a collaboration of voluntary and community organisations with funding from the Department for Education to provide reliable information to parents, teachers, schools and the wider sector. It acts as the important communication channel between government, leading dyslexia organisations, parents, schools, colleges, teachers and the sector.

www.thedyslexia-spldtrust.org.uk

Emerson House

Emerson House is a specialist centre for children aged 5 to 11. It offers assessment and teaching for dyscalculia, dyslexia and dyspraxia.

www.emersonhouse.co.uk

I CAN

I CAN is an educational charity for children with speech and language difficulties. It provides training and information for parents, teachers and therapists. It runs special school and nurseries and centres within local schools.

www.ican.org.uk

NASEN

NASEN (National Association for Special Educational Needs) promotes the education, training, advancement and development of all those with special and additional support needs.

www.nasen.org.uk

PATOSS

Patoss (Professional Association of Teachers of Students with Specific Learning Difficulties) represents the interests of teachers and students in matters that affect individuals with SpLD. It provides training and advice for teachers and maintains a directory of tutors and assessors.

www.patoss-dyslexia.org

Royal College of Speech and Language Therapists (RCSLT)

The RCSLT is the professional body for speech and language therapists in the UK. It provides information for members and the public about speech and language therapy.

www.rcslt.org

REFERENCES

Alloway, T.P. and Alloway, R.G. (2010) 'Investigating the predictive roles of working memory and IQ in academic attainment.' *Journal of Experimental Child Psychology 106*, 20–29.

American Heritage Dictionary (2011) *The American Heritage Dictionary of the English Language, Fifth Edition.* New York, NY: Houghton Mifflin Harcourt.

American Psychiatric Association (2013) *Diagnostic and Statistical Manual of Mental Disorders, Fifth Edition* (DSM-5). Arlington, VA: American Psychiatric Publishing.

Back, J. Sayers, J. and Andrews, P. (2014) 'The development of foundational number sense in England and Hungary: a case study comparison.' CERME – Eighth Congress of the European Society for Research in Mathematics Education, Antalya, Turkey, February 2013. Available at http://cerme8.metu.edu.tr/wgpapers/wg11_papers.html, accessed on 22 March 2015.

Boaler, J. (2009) *The Elephant in the Classroom: Helping Children Learn and Love Maths.* London: Souvenir Press.

Boaler, J. (2013) 'Ability and mathematics: the mindset revolution that is reshaping education.' *FORUM 55*, 1.

Butterworth, B. (1999) *The Mathematical Brain.* London: Macmillan.

Butterworth, B. and Kovas, Y. (2013) 'Understanding neurocognitive developmental disorders can improve education for all.' *Science 340*, 6130, 300–305.

Butterworth, B., Varma, S. and Laurillard, D. (2011) 'Dyscalculia: from brain to education.' *Science 332*, 6033, 1049–1053.

Center on the Developing Child (2004) *Enhancing and Practicing Executive Function Skills with Children from Infancy to Adolescence.* Harvard University website. Available at http://developingchild.harvard.edu/resources/tools_and_guides/enhancing_and_practicing_executive_function_skills_with_children, accessed on 17 February 2015.

Chinn, S. (2012) *More Trouble with Maths: A Complete Guide to Identifying and Diagnosing Mathematical Difficulties.* London: David Fulton/Nasen.

Chinn, S. and Ashcroft, R. (1993) *Mathematics for Dyslexics: A Teaching Handbook.* London: Whurr.

Clausen-May, T. (2013) *Teaching Mathematics Visually and Actively.* London: Sage Publications.

Cockcroft, W.H. (1982) Mathematics Counts: Report of the Committee of Inquiry into the Teaching of Mathematics in Schools under the Chairmanship of Dr WH Cockcroft. London: Her Majesty's Stationery Office.

Colker, R., Shaywitz, S., Shaywitz, B. and Simon, J.A. (2012) *Comments on Proposed DSM-5 Criteria for Specific Learning Disorder from a Legal and Medical/Scientific Perspective.* Available at http://dyslexia.yale.edu/POL_DSM5comments.html, accessed on 20 February 2015.

Dehaene, S. (1997) *The Number Sense: How the Mind Creates Mathematics.* Oxford: Oxford University Press.

Department for Education (2014) *National Curriculum in England: Mathematics Programmes of Study.* Statutory guidance. Available at www.gov.uk/government/publications/national-curriculum-in-england-mathematics-programmes-of-study/national-curriculum-in-england-mathematics-programmes-of-study, accessed on 18 February 2015.

Department for Education and Skills (2001) *Guidance to Support Pupils with Dyslexia and Dyscalculia (DfES 0521/2001).* London: DfES.

Department for Education and Department of Health (2015) *Special Educational Needs and Disability Code of Practice: 0 to 25 Years.* Available at www.gov.uk/government/uploads/system/uploads/attachment_data/file/398815/SEND_Code_of_Practice_January_2015.pdf, accessed on 15 February 2015.

Dweck, C.S. (2006) *Mindset: The New Psychology of Success.* New York, NY: Random House.

Dyscalculia Screener (n.d.) *Dyscalculia Screener.* Available at www.gl-assessment.co.uk/products/dyscalculia-screener, accessed on 20 February 2015.

DysCalculiUM (n.d.) DysCalculiUM. Available at https://shop.tribalgroup.co.uk/vmchk/Assessment-screening/DyscalculiUM.html, accessed on 20 February 2015.

Emerson, J. and Babtie, P. (2013) *The Dyscalculia Assessment.* London: Bloomsbury.

Emerson, J. and Babtie, P. (2014) *The Dyscalculia Solution: Teaching Number Sense.* London: Bloomsbury.

Encyclopedia of Children's Health (n.d.) *Beery-Buktenica Test.* Available at www.healthofchildren.com/B/Beery-Buktenica-Test.html, accessed on 18 February 2015.

Gathercole, S.E. and Alloway, T.P. (2007) *Understanding Memory: A Classroom Guide.* London: Harcourt Assessment. Available at www.york.ac.uk/res/wml/Classroom%20guide.pdf, accessed on 18 February 2015.

Gelman, R. and Gallistel, C.R. (1978) *The Child's Understanding of Number.* Cambridge, MA: Harvard University Press.

Hopkins, G. (2004) *How Can Teachers Develop Students' Motivation – and Success?* Education World website. Available at www.educationworld.com/a_issues/chat/chat010.shtml#sthash.UKxS650X.dpuf, accessed 17 February 2015.

Kirby, A. (2006) *Dyspraxia: Developmental Co-ordination Disorder.* London: Souvenir Press.

Lee, A. (2014) *How IDEA Protects You and Your Child.* Available at www.understood.org/en/school-learning/your-childs-rights/basics-about-childs-rights/how-idea-protects-you-and-your-child, accessed on 22 March 2015.

Maats, H. and O'Brien, K. (2013) *The Straight-A Conspiracy: Your Secret Guide to Ending the Stress of School and Totally Ruling the World.* Los Angeles, CA: 368 Press

Mareschal, D., Butterworth, B. and Tolmie, A. (2013) *Educational Neuroscience.* Chichester: Wiley Blackwell.

Maudsley, H. (1874) 'Sex in mind and education.' *Popular Science Month,* 5, 198–215.

Morin, A. (2014) *Understanding Executive Functioning Issues.* Understood website. Available at www.understood.org/en/learning-attention-issues/child-learning-disabilities/executive-functioning-issues/understanding-executive-functioning-issues, accessed on 17 February 2015.

National Numeracy (2013) *What Is Numeracy?* Available at www.nationalnumeracy. org.uk/what-is-numeracy/index.html, accessed on 13 March 2015.

NGA (2010) *Common Core State Standards.* Washington, DC: National Governors Association Center for Best Practices, Council of Chief State School Officers. 2015.

NICE (National Institute for Health and Care Excellence) (2013) *Attention Deficit Hyperactivity Disorder: Diagnosis and Management of ADHD in Children, Young People and Adults.* Clinical guideline 72. Available at www.nice.org.uk/ guidance/cg72, accessed on 17 February 2015.

OECD (n.d.) *Programme for International Student Assessment (PISA).* Available at www. oecd.org/pisa/aboutpisa, accessed on 17 February 2015.

Portwood, M. (2000) *Understanding Developmental Dyspraxia: A Textbook for Students and Professionals.* London: David Fulton.

Rose, J. (2009) *Identifying and Teaching Children and Young People with Dyslexia and Literacy Difficulties: An Independent Report from Sir Jim Rose to the Secretary of State for Children, Schools and Families.* Available at http://webarchive. nationalarchives.gov.uk/20130401151715/http://www.education.gov.uk/ publications/eOrderingDownload/00659-2009DOM-EN.pdf, accessed on 15 March 2015.

Rosenstein, J.G., Caldwell, and J. H. Crown W.D. (1996) 'New Jersey Mathematics Curriculum Framework.' New Jersey Mathematics Coalition and the New Jersey Department of Education. http://www.state.nj.us/education/archive/ frameworks/math/math.pdf. Accessed 12 June 2015

Sensory Processing Disorder Foundation (2014) *About SPD.* Available at http:// spdfoundation.net/about-sensory-processing-disorder.html, accessed on 13 March 2015.

Sharron, H. and Coulter, M. (1987) *Changing Children's Minds: Feuerstein's Revolution in the Teaching of Intelligence.* Digbeth: Imaginative Minds.

Simmons, F.R. (2011) 'Mathematics difficulties: current research and future directions'. *Dyslexia Review 22,* 1, 18–19.

Strauss, V. (2013) Howard Gardner: 'Multiple intelligences' are not 'learning styles'. Interview. Available at www.washingtonpost.com/blogs/answer-sheet/ wp/2013/10/16/howard-gardner-multiple-intelligences-are-not-learning- styles, accessed on 17 February 2015.

Suzman, H. (1993). *In No Uncertain Terms.* Cape Town: Jonathan Ball.

Van den Heuvel-Panhuizen, M. (2001) *Realistic Mathematics Education as Work in Progress.* Available at www.fisme.science.uu.nl/staff/marjah/documents/ Marja_Work-in-progress.pdf, accessed on 19 February 2015.

West, T.G. (2009) *In the Mind's Eye.* New York: Prometheus Books.

World Health Organization (2010) *The International Classification of Diseases 10 (ICD-10) Classification of Mental and Behavioural Disorders: Clinical Descriptions and Diagnostic Guidelines.* Geneva: WHO Publications.

Young, C.B., Wu, S.S. and Menon, V. (2012) 'The neurodevelopmental basis of math anxiety.' *Psychological Science 23,* 492–501.

FURTHER READING

Anghilieri, J. (2006) *Teaching Number Sense* (2nd edn). London: Continuum.

Anghilieri, J. (2007) *Developing Number Sense.* London: Continuum.

Askew, M. *et al.* (2001) *Raising attainment in Primary Number Sense: From Counting to Strategy.* London: BEAM Education.

Ashlock, R.B. (2006) *Error Patterns in Computation.* New Jersey: Pearson Merrill Prentice Hall.

Bird, R. (2007) *The Dyscalculia Toolkit: Supporting Learning Difficulties in Maths.* London: Paul Chapman.

Butterworth, B. and Yeo, D. (2004) *Dyscalculia Guidance.* London: Nelson.

Chinn, S. (2004) *The Trouble with Maths.* Abingdon: Routledge Falmer.

Dowker, A. (2009) *What Works for Children with Mathematical Difficulties? The Effectiveness of Intervention Schemes.* Reference 00086-2009BKT-EN. London: The National Archives.

Gardner, H. (2011) *Frames of Mind: The Theory of Multiple Intelligences.* New York: Basic Books.

Gattengno, C. (1963) *Now Johnny Can Do Arithmetic: A Handbook on the Use of Cuisenaire Rods.* Reading: Educational Explorers.

Gifford, S. and Rockliffe, F. (2012) 'Mathematics difficulties: does one approach fit all?' *Research in Mathematics Education 14*, 1, 1–15.

Gifford, S. (2005) *Young Children's Difficulties in Learning Mathematics: Review of Research in Relation to Dyscalculia.* London: Qualifications and Curriculum Authority.

Grauberg, E. (1998) *Elementary Mathematics and Language Difficulties.* London: Whurr.

Henderson, A. (2012) *Dyslexia, Dyscalculia and Mathematics: A Practical Guide.* London: Routledge.

Howard, S. and Coulter, M. (1996) *Changing Children's Minds: Feuerstein's Revolution in the Teaching of Intelligence.* Birmingham: Imaginative Minds.

Nash-Wortham, M. and Hunt, J. (1997) *Take Time.* Stourbridge: Robinswood Press.

Thompson, I, (1999) *Issues in Teaching Numeracy in Primary Schools.* Buckingham: Open University Press.

Wilson, A. (2004) *Dyscalculia Primer and Resource Guide.* OECD, Directorate for Education website. Available at www.oecd.org/document/8/0,3343,en_2649_35845581_34495560_1_1_1_1,00.html, accessed 17 February 2015.

Yeo, D. (2003) *Dyslexia, Dyspraxia and Mathematics.* London: Whurr.

INDEX